First Steps in SAP® ABAP® RESTful Application Programming Model (RAP)

Julian Danho
Phillip Dörrschuck

Thank you for purchasing this book from Espresso Tutorials!

Like a cup of espresso coffee, Espresso Tutorials SAP books are concise and effective. We know that your time is valuable and we deliver information in a succinct and straightforward manner. It only takes our readers a short amount of time to consume SAP concepts. Our books are well recognized in the industry for leveraging tutorial-style instruction and videos to show you step by step how to successfully work with SAP.

Check out our YouTube channel to watch our videos at *https://www.youtube.com/user/EspressoTutorials*.

If you are interested in SAP Finance and Controlling, please join us at *https://forum.espresso-tutorials.com/* to get your SAP questions answered and contribute to discussions.

Related titles from Espresso Tutorials:

- Prem Manghnani, Seshu Reddy & Sheshank Vyas:
  Practical Guide to SAP® OpenUI5
  http://5148.espresso-tutorials.com
- Robert Burdwell:
  First Steps for Building SAP®UI5 Mobile Apps
  http://5176.espresso-tutorials.com
- Gretchen Horn:
  Practical Guide to SAP® Workflow Agent Determination
  http://5200.espresso-tutorials.com
- Marco Verhoef:
  A Practical Guide to the SAP® Cloud Connector
  http://5509.espresso-tutorials.com
- Adam Kiwon:
  A Practical Guide to SAP® Cloud Integration
  http://5651.espresso-tutorials.com
- Boris Rubarth:
  First Steps in SAP ABAP®—2nd edition
  https://es-tu.de/nKfwhx

Julian Danho, Phillip Dörrschuck
First Steps in SAP® ABAP® RESTful Application Programming Model (RAP)

ISBN: 978-3-960124-91-7

Editor: Karen Schoch

Cover Design: Philip Esch, Olesia Donchenko

Cover Photo: iStockphoto.com | carloscastilla No. 1250534724

Interior Book Design: Johann-Christian Hanke

1st Edition 2025, Gleichen

URL: *www.espresso-tutorials.com*

Feedback
We greatly appreciate any feedback you may have concerning this book. Please send your feedback via email to: *info@espresso-tutorials.com*.

Table of Contents

Foreword

We are delighted to present this book, which offers you an insight into the fascinating world of the ABAP RESTful Application Programming Model (RAP).

As developers, we know that change can be challenging. Questioning familiar work methods and technologies, and embracing something new requires courage and openness. The previous programming models were familiar to us, and we were initially reluctant to make the switch to RAP. We can now say that we are strong advocates of the new programming mode, and no longer want to work with SEGW/BOPF.

We encourage you to openly engage with the RAP model and actively explore the concepts covered in this book. Practical examples and exercises will help you to experience RAP through real-life applications and gain a deeper understanding of it.

Switching to RAP may be challenging at first, but we are confident that your efforts will pay off. With the deployment of SAP S/4HANA, the RAP model is becoming increasingly important and offers the opportunity to develop innovative and future-proof solutions.

Who is this book for?

This book is aimed at ABAP developers and consultants with basic ABAP knowledge who are looking for a practice-oriented introduction to the RAP model. Previous knowledge of CDS (core data services) would also be an advantage.

For newcomers to RAP, we offer a solid foundation for successfully applying this model to your own projects.

For experienced developers, we present innovative approaches and proven solutions to unlock the full potential of RAP.

Our aim is to provide a practical and in-depth guide that will enable you to successfully develop complex applications while ensuring the maintainability and extensibility of your solutions.

Structure and content

This book is carefully structured and offers an in-depth insight into SAP's RAP model. We have designed it to guide you step-by-step through the various features and potential of this model.

Chapter 1 forms the basis for understanding the RAP model. It deals with the background and motivation behind this book, as well as the evolution of the ABAP programming model. We guide you through basic concepts in order to create a solid foundation.

Chapter 2 deals with configuration and the prerequisites needed to understand and follow the exercises in this book. We discuss system requirements and explain the ABAP Flight Reference Model as an essential basis for the subsequent chapters.

Chapter 3 delves into the basics of the ABAP RESTful Application Programming Model. We start with an introduction to the framework before moving on to specific components such as business objects, their behavior definition and implementation, and business services. Each section is illustrated with practical examples.

Chapter 4 is dedicated to Entity Manipulation Language (EML), which is the new appendix to ABAP programming language. We cover various use cases and show you how to read, update and create data in ABAP using the RAP model. This chapter is crucial for understanding how to interact with data in the RAP model.

In Chapter 5, we explore different methodologies in RAP, such as numbering, determinations, validations, actions, functions, unmanaged saves, drafts, and hierarchies. You will learn how to use these methods to develop powerful and reliable applications.

Chapter 6 introduces you to the world of custom entities. We explain the design and implementation, as well as the advantages and disadvantages of these flexible data structures. You will learn how to use custom entities to filter and aggregate data effectively.

This structured guide will help you to comprehensively master the SAP RAP model and successfully implement it in your projects. We wish you an insightful read and every success on your journey through the exciting world of SAP development.

☛ Git repository for this book

You can find the codes for this book in our Git repository:

https://github.com/jp-devops-hub/rap-book (Chapters 1–5), and

https://github.com/jp-devops-hub/rap-book-customentity (Chapter 6)

We have added a few icons to highlight important information. These include:

Tip

Tips highlight information that provides more details about the subject being described and/or additional background information.

Example

Examples help illustrate a topic better by relating it to real world scenarios.

! Attention

Attention notices highlight information that you should be aware of when you go through the examples in this book on your own.

Finally, a note concerning the copyright: all SAP product screenshots printed in this book are the copyright of SAP SE. All rights are reserved by SAP SE. Copyright pertains to all SAP images in this publication. All other trademarks are the property of their respective owners. For the sake of simplicity, we do not mention this specifically underneath every screenshot.

1 Introduction

Welcome to the world of the third generation of the ABAP programming model for SAP S/4HANA. The innovative ABAP RESTful Application Programming Model (RAP) plays a crucial role in modern SAP development. In an age of S/4HANA, where the requirements for business applications and data processing are rapidly evolving, RAP offers a future-oriented solution. This introduction chapter lays the foundation for a deeper understanding of the changes and opportunities offered by S/4HANA and RAP. It takes you on a journey through the evolution of ABAP programming and shows how SAP developers can adapt and leverage the new technologies to create efficient, scalable and user-friendly applications.

In this chapter, we explore the evolution of ABAP programming to RAP for S/4HANA, a modern method for developing efficient, REST-based applications that fully utilize the capabilities of S/4HANA.

The evolution of the ABAP programming model reflects technological progress and adaptation to the needs of the modern business world. RAP integrates proven technologies such as CDS, ABAP and SAPUI5 to create an efficient and structured development environment.

1.1 Background and motivation

The introduction of SAP S/4HANA fundamentally changed ABAP development. With S/4HANA, SAP created a new generation of software that is based on simplified database architecture and offers a range of functions and options.

Traditional ABAP development approaches are reaching their limits when it comes to benefiting from the advantages of S/4HANA. The introduction of RAP is SAP's response to these challenges.

S/4HANA enables simplified data modeling with the CDS framework, an improved user interface featuring SAP Fiori, and efficient processing of business logic.

With RAP, you can get the most out of S/4HANA in terms of performance, scalability and user experience. Modern, cloud-enabled applications can be developed, that seamlessly integrate into the system landscape and generate added value for companies.

1.2 Evolution of the ABAP programming model

The ABAP programming model has evolved over time to meet the growing needs of the business world (see Figure 1.1). The evolutionary stages reflect technological advances and changing application development requirements.

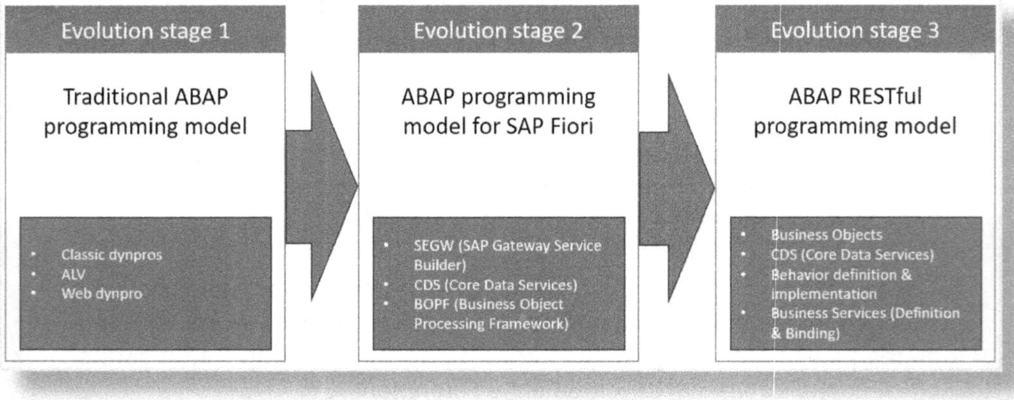

Figure 1.1: ABAP evolution

1.2.1 Evolution stage 1—Traditional ABAP programming model

SAP did not initially specify a standardized procedure for the development of applications. Instead, developers followed the principle of best-practice freestyle ABAP programming. This enabled them to use different technologies such as ABAP, Dynpro, Web Dynpro, BSP, among others, as they wished. This freedom made work easier, but led to medium-term disadvantages.

Because there was no standardized model, new developers had to get themselves thoroughly acquainted with the heterogeneous technological landscape in order to make changes to existing systems. There were no standards, which meant wasted time and money that would have been better spent on development.

1.2.2 Evolution stage 2—ABAP programming model for SAP Fiori

With the introduction of SAP NetWeaver 7.4, SAP began to optimize the ABAP platform for the HANA database. In this context, CDS, SAP Gateway and OData were made available to customers. The introduction of SAP Fiori created a new user experience, and the variety of technologies continued to increase.

To meet SAP Fiori application requirements and ensure a high level of product quality and simple lifecycle management, SAP introduced the ABAP programming model for SAP Fiori. This model enabled scalable and maintainable applications that were ready for the cloud. This facilitated the onboarding of new developers, as they no longer had to work their way through extensive documentation.

The ABAP programming model for SAP Fiori was based on proven technologies such as CDS, BOPF and SAP Gateway. This made it possible to develop transactional and analytical applications. The model consisted of different layers, including SAPUI5 for user interfaces, OData as the communication protocol, ABAP for business logic, and CDS for data models. This made it possible to create a standardized development environment.

1.2.3 Evolution stage 3—ABAP RESTful Application Programming Model (RAP)

RAP is the latest stage of the evolution of the ABAP programming model. It was developed to enable efficient web-based applications and WEB APIs.

RAP is based on the ABAP programming model for SAP Fiori and integrates various technologies such as CDS, ABAP and SAPUI5. It offers a standardized and efficient development environment that reduces development costs and provides developers with a clear structure and tools.

Throughout the evolution of the ABAP programming model, SAP has worked continuously to modernize ABAP development and meet the changing needs of the business world. Each evolutionary stage has led to improved development possibilities, higher product quality and better scalability of applications.

2 Configuration

Before jumping deeper into RAP, we first need to check whether your SAP system meets all the requirements to operate smoothly. In this chapter, we are going to carry out all the necessary configurations, step by step.

This chapter focuses on the requirements for effective ABAP development in SAP S/4HANA, especially for RAP. We discuss the basic system requirements, the installation of Eclipse with ABAP Development Tools, and SAP GUI (graphical user interface). A significant amount of this chapter is dedicated to the ABAP Flight Reference Model—a central element for practical exercises. We include step-by-step instructions for checking the package status, downloading and setting up the model, and installing abapGit in order to import the package. After successful preparation and installation, you can jump straight into the practical exercises and examples.

> **ABAP Flight Reference Model**
>
> The ABAP Flight Reference Model is a database model used in SAP systems, that has been specially designed for training purposes. It comprises a collection of relational database tables containing "flight data", "bookings", and "passenger information". The exercises in this book are based on this model. More information can be found under: *https://help.sap.com/docs/ABAP_PLATFORM_NEW/fc4c71aa50014fd1b43721701471913d/a9d7c7c140a0408dbc5966c52d156b49.html?locale=en-US.*

2.1 Prerequisites

2.1.1 SAP system

The development exercises presented in this book are possible as of S/4HANA On-Premise 2021 release. To ensure unproblematic performance of the exercises, we strongly recommend using this version or a newer one. In addition, it is necessary that you have a valid development key and access to an SAP system within your company. These prerequisites are essential in order to take full advantage of the exercises and make the most of the content in this book.

2.1.2 Required software

For optimal performance of the exercises in this book, it is important that your computer is equipped with some specific software tools. We recommend installing:

1. *Eclipse*—an integrated development environment that enables efficient programming (*https://www.eclipse.org/downloads/*)
2. *ABAP Development Tools (ADT)*—an indispensable toolkit for development with ABAP in the Eclipse environment (*https://tools.hana.ondemand.com/#abap*)
3. *SAP GUI*

> **External links—important note**
>
> Note that the URLs given in this book were current at the time of writing. However, it is possible that web addresses may change over time. If you encounter problems accessing the links, we recommend searching the relevant keywords (such as *Eclipse Download* or *ABAP Development Tools*) using your favorite search engine to find the latest valid web pages.

2.2 ABAP Flight Reference Model

Once you have met the prerequisites the next step is to check whether the ABAP Flight Reference Model, on which the exercises in this book are based, is installed on your system.

2.2.1 Checking the parcel status

To check whether the required packages are available on your system, start a search in Eclipse using the flashlight button (). This opens the ABAP

OBJECT SEARCH. In this window, enter the package name */DMO/** in the OBJECT NAME PATTERN field ❶ and click on SEARCH ❷ (see Figure 2.1).

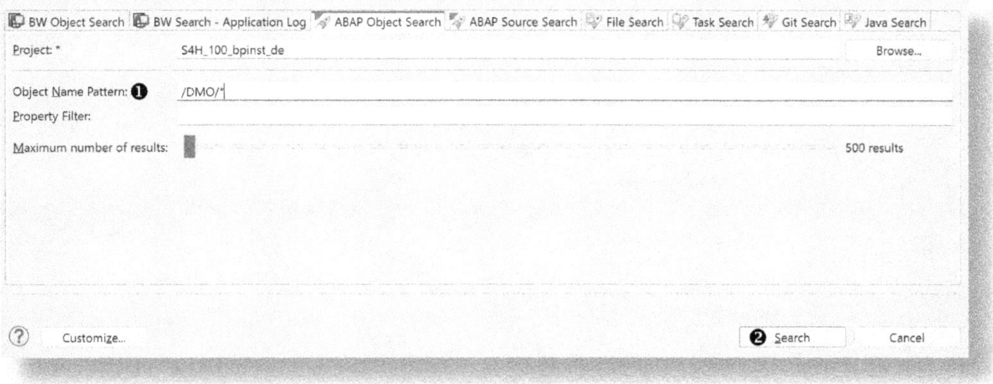

Figure 2.1: ABAP Object Search window

Once the search has been completed, Eclipse will display any elements that have been found. If there are none, as shown in Figure 2.2, you need to install the package. If packages are found during the search, the installation steps in Chapter 2 can be skipped and you can proceed directly with the instructions from Chapter 3; this is because the /DMO/ package is already installed within the SAP system.

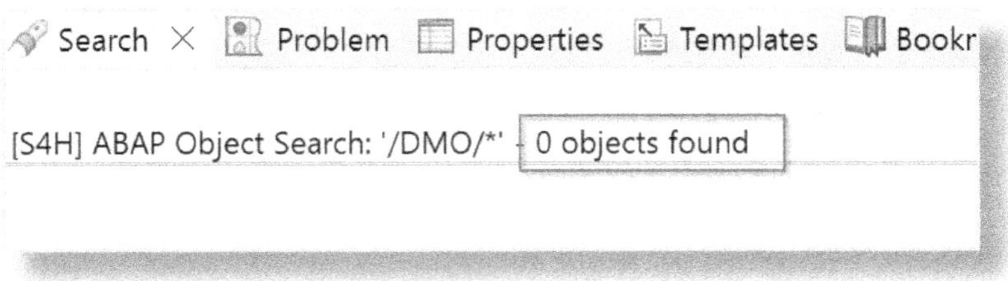

Figure 2.2: ABAP Object Search—result

2.2.2 Downloading the package

The model is provided as an abapGit package on the official SAP GitHub repository. The repository can be found at *https://github.com/SAP-samples/abap-platform-refscen-flight*.

On this page, select the relevant Git branch for your current backend release (see Figure 2.3).

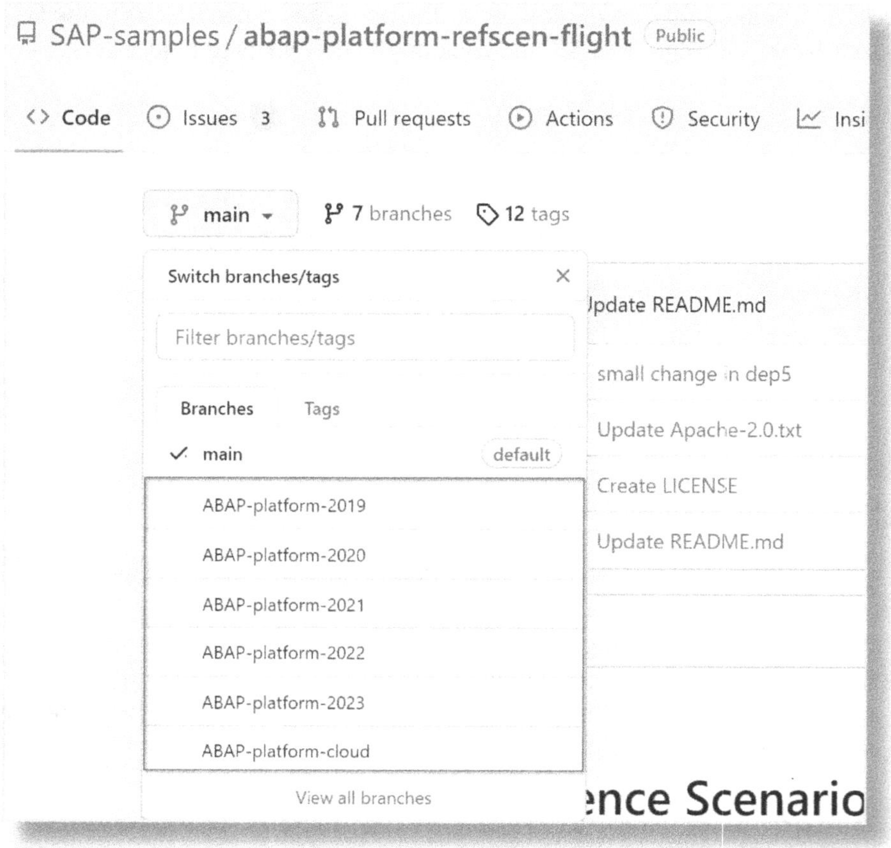

Figure 2.3: Available versions

After downloading the required branch as a ZIP file, you need to set up the namespace before installing the package.

! Namespace configuration

Before proceeding, ensure that you are on a training or sandbox system. The configuration of namespaces is a central setting, so you need comprehensive authorizations in your system. It may therefore be necessary for a qualified SAP Basis administrator from your company to carry out the configuration shown here.

2.2.3 Setting up a namespace

Before the /DMO/ package can be imported, a namespace must be set up. To do this, open transaction *SE03* (Transport Organizer Tools). Select ADMINISTRATION • DISPLAY/CHANGE NAMESPACES from the menu.

A client-independent table then opens, in which you can create a new entry (see Figure 2.4).

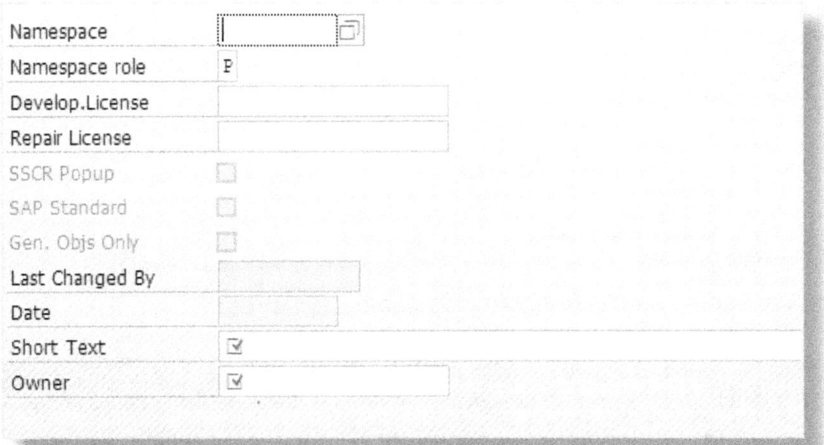

Figure 2.4: Maintaining a new namespace

The values for the new namespace can be found in the GitHub repository under the system-specific branch in the README.md file, where you will find the SET UP NAMESPACE section (see Figure 2.5).

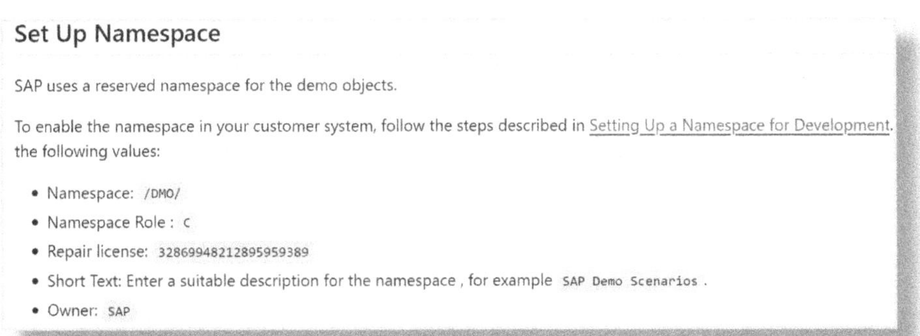

Figure 2.5: /DMO/ namespace—values

Once you have entered the values, you can save them and return to the transaction *SE03* menu. Changeability for the `/DMO/ namespace` must now be set. To do this, select ADMINISTRATION • SET SYSTEM CHANGE OPT from the menu.

In the displayed table maintenance view, search for the prefix /DMO/ and set the status to *Modifiable* (see Figure 2.6).

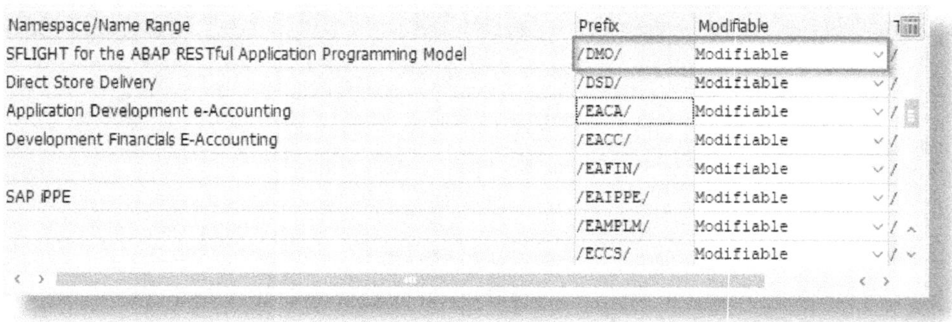

Figure 2.6: Setting prefix /DMO/ to modifiable

> **! Always follow instructions in the README.md file**
>
> Note that further preparatory work might be necessary, which we were not able to fully cover in this book. Make sure to carefully review the README.md file in the repository before proceeding to the next step.

2.2.4 Installing abapGit

To import the package into your system, you need abapGit.

You can download the source code for abapGit from the official site, at: *https://docs.abapgit.org/*.

Under WELCOME TO ABAPGIT, you will find the latest published version of the program, as shown in Figure 2.7.

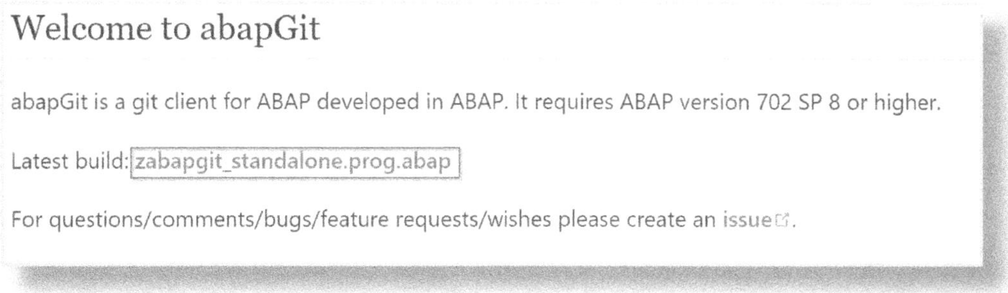

Figure 2.7: Latest version of abapGit

Click on the link to display the source text in raw format. Before loading this into the system via copy-and-paste, you need to create an ABAP program. To do this, switch to Eclipse and right-click on the system to open the create dialog box. Select NEW • OTHER... from the context menu, as shown in Figure 2.8.

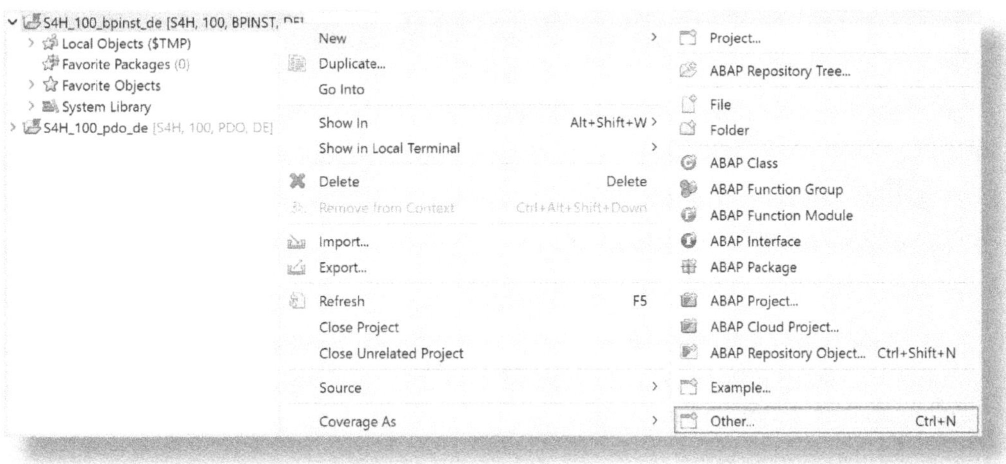

Figure 2.8: Creating new object

In the dialog box that opens, search for ABAP PROGRAM ❶ and confirm by clicking on NEXT ❷ (see Figure 2.9).

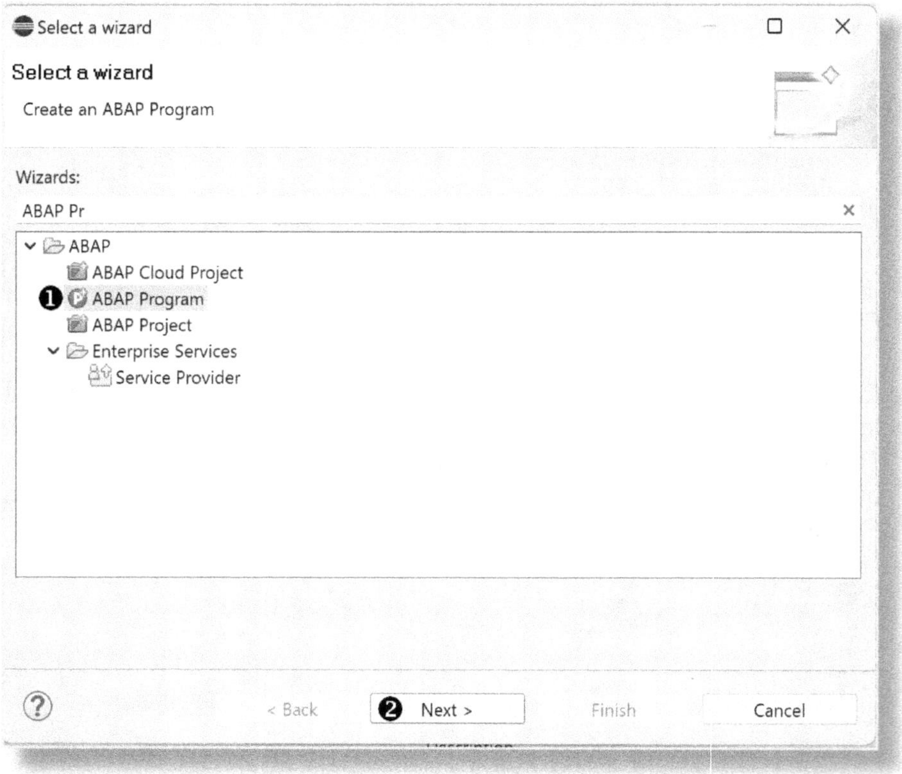

Figure 2.9: Select "ABAP program"

Referring to Figure 2.10, select the *$TMP* as the PACKAGE ❶ (local developments, without transport) and enter *ZABAPGIT_STANDALONE* ❷ as the program NAME. Enter a DESCRIPTION ❸ and then confirm the installation by clicking on the FINISH button ❹

Next, copy the source code (see Figure 2.11) from the browser using `Ctrl` + `C` and paste it into the ABAP program using `Ctrl` + `V`. The source code shown here can be found on the abapGit website (see Figure 2.7). Due to the size of the program, the copying process may take some time.

Now, activate the program by clicking on the button, and run it by pressing the function key `F8`.

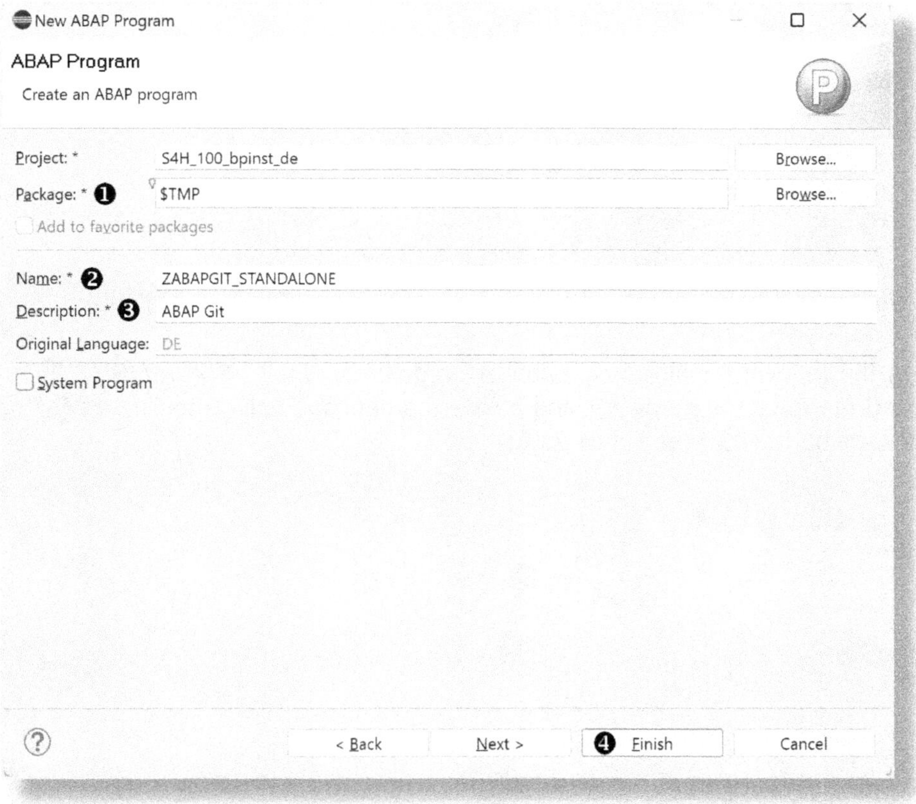

Figure 2.10: Enter information on the program installation

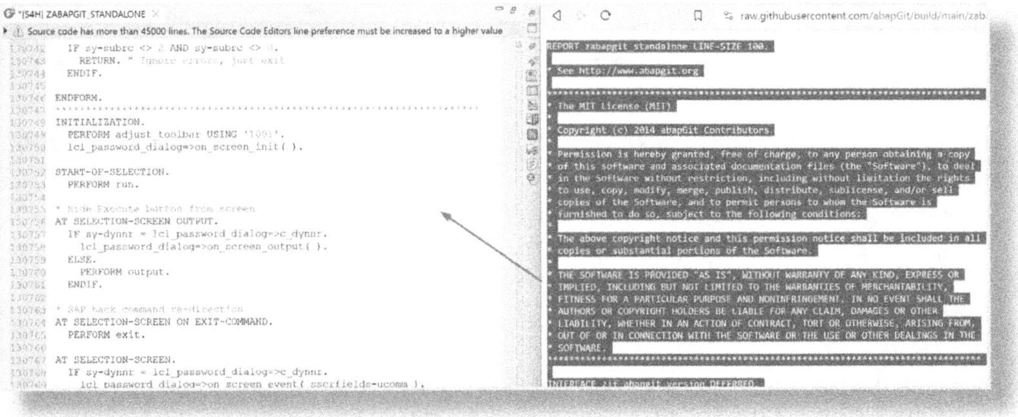

Figure 2.11: Copying program code

2.2.5 Importing the package

You can now import the downloaded ZIP file via abapGit. To do this, click on the NEW OFFLINE button in the menu bar (see Figure 2.12).

Figure 2.12: New offline package

In the following dialog box, enter the repository NAME */DMO/FLIGHT* ❶ and the PACKAGE name ❷ and create the package using the CREATE PACKAGE button ❸ (see Figure 2.13).

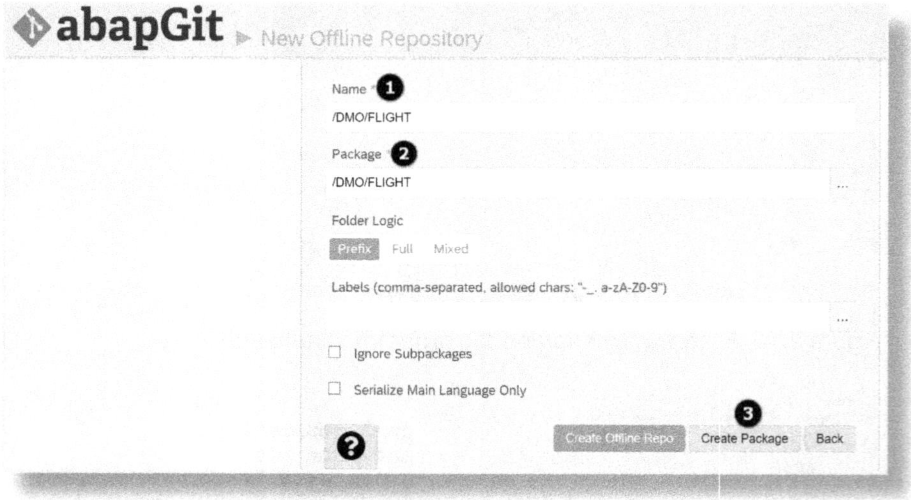

Figure 2.13: Creating a package

A new dialog box then opens, where you create the package in the SAP system (see Figure 2.14). Enter a SHORT DESCRIPTION ❶ for the package and assign it to a SOFTWARE COMPONENT ❷. Confirm your entries by clicking on the ✓ button ❸.

Once the package has been created, it is the repository's turn. Click on the CREATE OFFLINE REPO button (see Figure 2.15).

The new repository is displayed, and you can import the ZIP file from your computer into the SAP system using the IMPORT ZIP button (see Figure 2.16).

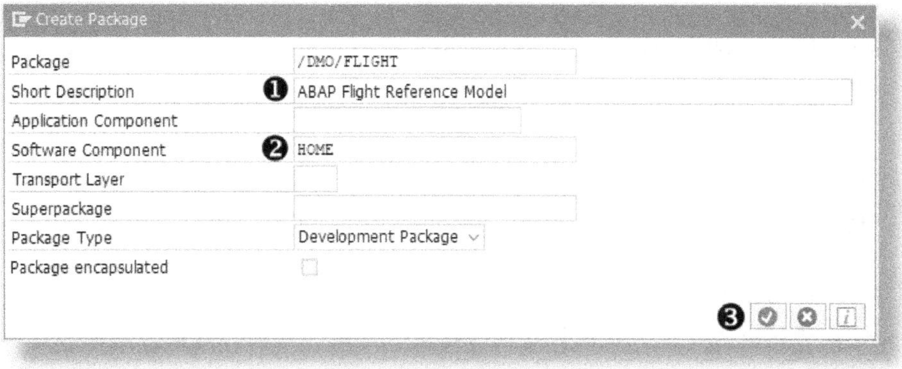

Figure 2.14: Creating the package "/DMO/FLIGHT"

Figure 2.15: Creating a repository

Figure 2.16: Importing ZIP file

Click to open the operating system dialog box for opening files. As shown in Figure 2.17, select the file downloaded from the GitHub repository and click on the OPEN button.

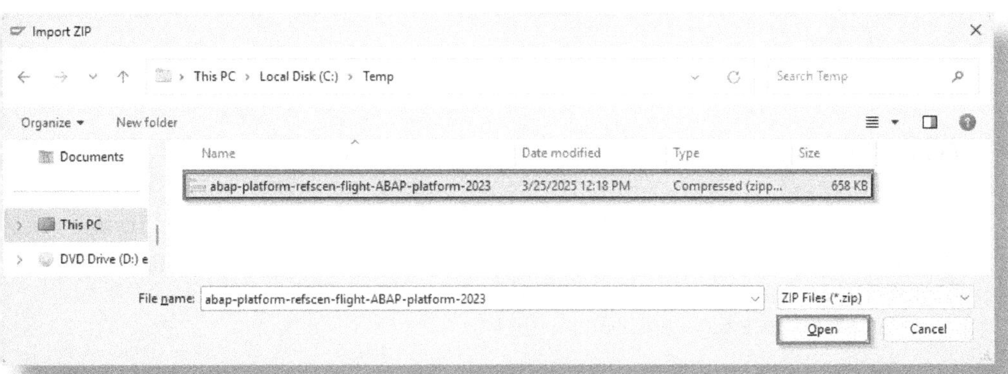

Figure 2.17: Selecting the file on the operating system

After abapGit has serialized all the files, the PULL ZIP button appears in the overview (see Figure 2.18). Click on it to start importing the elements.

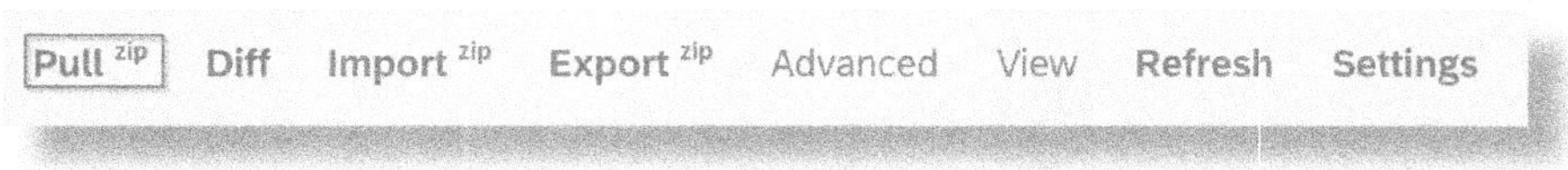

Figure 2.18: Pulling the changes

First, a dialog box appears, listing all the elements to be imported. Confirm by clicking on the ✓ button (see Figure 2.19).

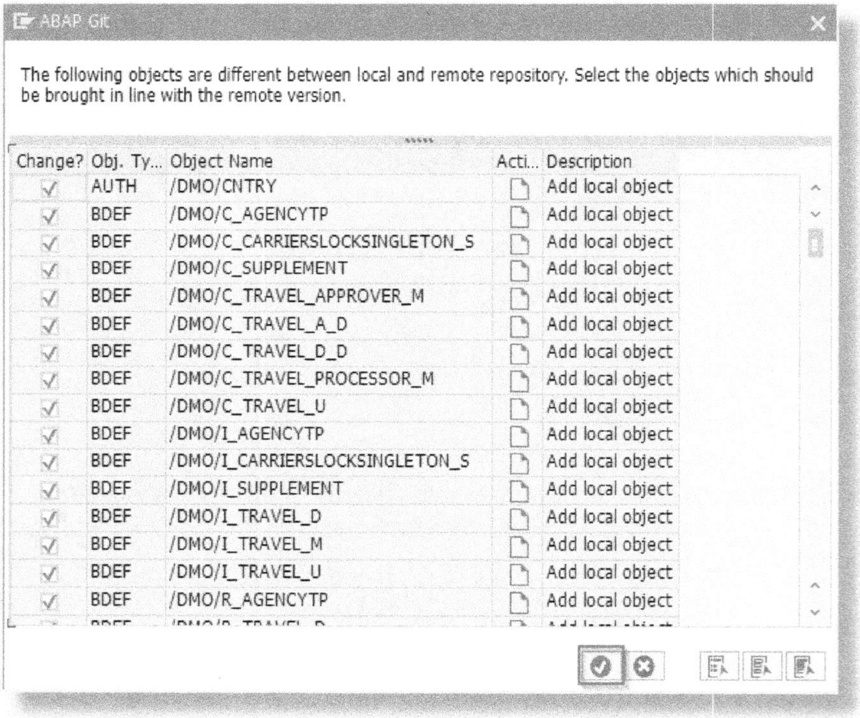

Figure 2.19: Importing elements

After successful import, fill the created database tables with data. To do this, open the /DMO/FLIGHT_LEGACY package in Eclipse and navigate to SOURCE CODE LIBRARY • CLASSES • /DMO/CL_FLIGHT_DATA_GENERATOR in the menu tree (see Figure 2.20).

Double-click on the class, and to execute it as a console application, use function button F9. Alternatively, you can click on the execute button (▶), as shown in Figure 2.21.

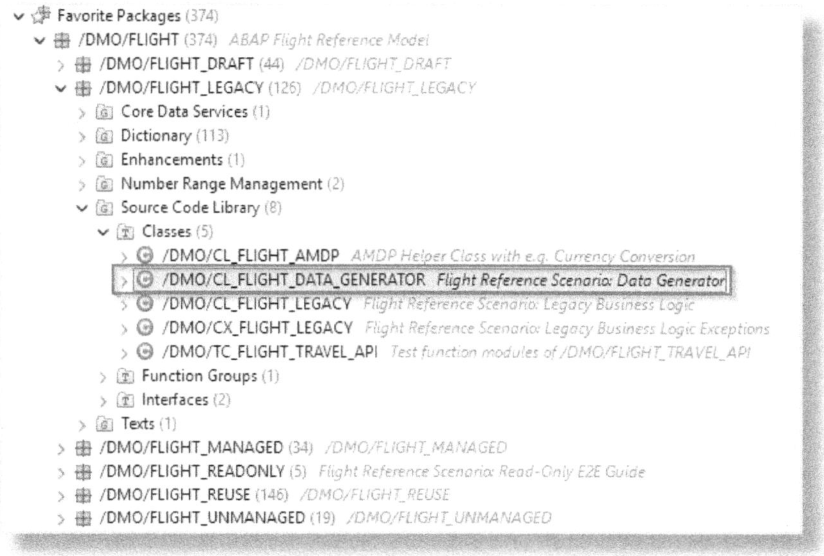

Figure 2.20: Class "Data generator"

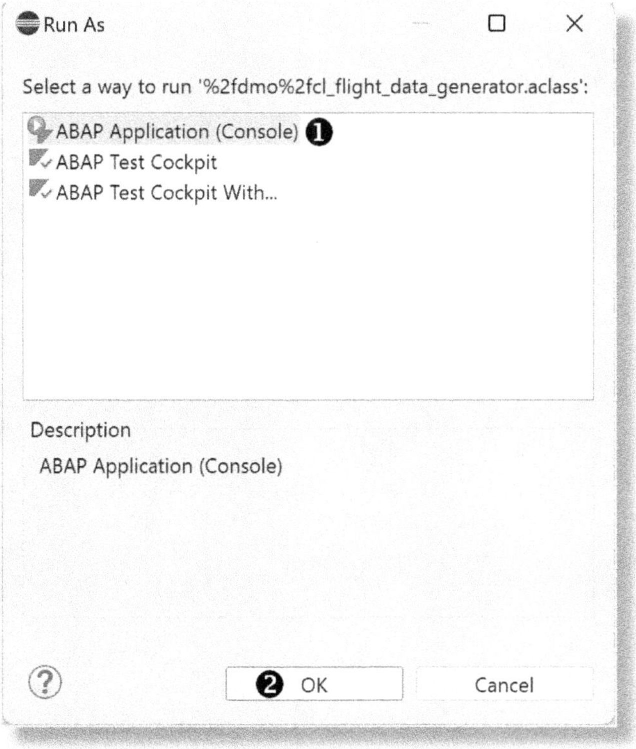

Figure 2.21: Executing class "Data generator"

Select option ABAP APPLICATION (CONSOLE) ❶ and confirm the selection by clicking on OK ❷.

If the execution is successful, a message appears in the console—FINISHED DATA GENERATION—as shown in Figure 2.22.

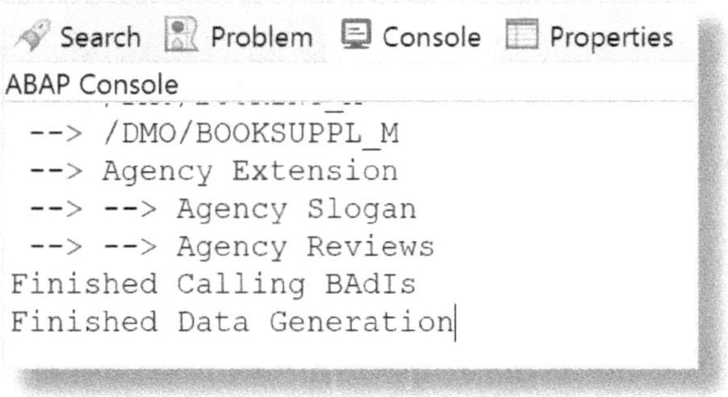

Figure 2.22: Success message after data generation

3 ABAP RESTful Application Programming Model—the basics

In this chapter, we dive into the basics of the ABAP RESTful Application Programming Model (RAP) and lay the foundation for a solid understanding.

We start with a detailed introduction to the RAP model and explain the architecture behind this approach. We illustrate the key concepts and principles that make the model so powerful and flexible. As a result, you will develop a clear understanding of how RAP is structured.

The rest of the chapter is dedicated to creating a RAP model. We guide you through the process, step by step, and explain each of the created components in detail.

> **Initial Fiori application**
>
> In this chapter, you will develop your first Fiori list report application in the RAP model. This application contains all the transactional functions such as creating, editing and deleting. Automatic filters and sorting options are also offered.

We believe that it is very important to understand not only the technical implementation, but also the underlying concepts. We therefore explain each step in detail to ensure that you fully grasp the basic principles of the RAP model.

By the end of this chapter, you will have not only created a functional model but also developed a solid understanding of its architecture and functionality. This forms the basis for further steps into the world of RAP.

3.1 Introduction to RAP

3.1.1 The three main players

RAP is based on three main components that pave the way for efficient and flexible application development:

1. **ABAP Development Tools in Eclipse for all development tasks**—the Eclipse development environment makes it easier for developers to get started and supports the entire development process.
2. **ABAP and CDS**—the combination of ABAP and core data services (CDS) enables standardized implementation tasks and efficient development.
3. **Frameworks**—the RAP model takes on technical implementation tasks and enables the integration of business logic in code-based exits.

Thanks to these main components, the RAP model provides a robust basis for modern application architecture.

3.1.2 Three-layer architecture

RAP consists of a three-layer architecture for efficient end-to-end development of OData services specifically optimized for SAP HANA, including Fiori apps. It provides developers with an efficient way to create enterprise-ready, OData-based Fiori UI (user interface) services and web APIs.

As part of development with RAP, we apply a bottom-up approach. The key components of this approach are illustrated in Figure 3.1, which shows the main development artifacts for creating an OData service within a three-layer architecture. These components and their functions in the development process are explained in more detail below.

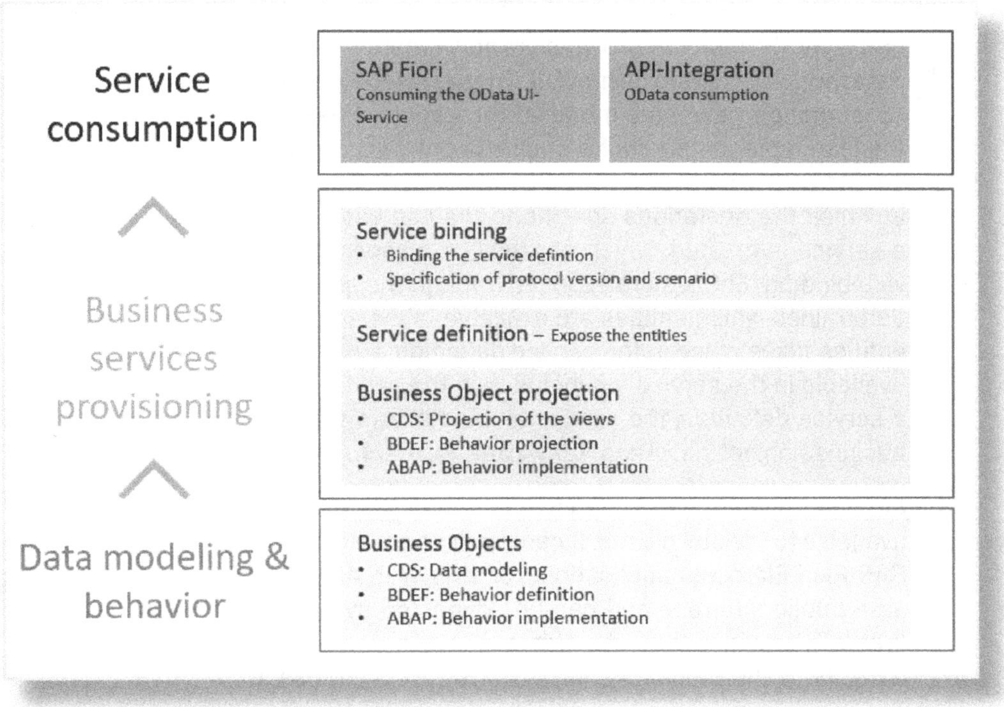

Figure 3.1: Three-layer architecture

This image shows the main development artifacts for creating an OData service within a three-layer architecture. These components and their functions in the development process are as follows:

1. **Data modeling & behavior**—in this layer, the data model that forms the basis is defined. This involves modeling *entities* for a business scenario. In the ABAP Flight Reference Model, this would be the equivalent of a trip or a booking. Entities can have relationships with each other; for example, a trip can contain several bookings. In this case, we would have a parent-child relationship. Core data services (CDS) are used to model the data model, and these are used to create *view entities*. These play a central role in RAP. Behavior is defined for a view entity. This contains the operations that can be performed on the data, such as CRUD (create, read, update, and delete) operations, actions, functions, etc. These behaviors are implemented with ABAP.

2. **Business services provisioning**—based on the data models from the first layer, the *projected objects* are now created. A restricted view of the data model is created using CDS. These *projection views* (also known as *consumption views*) are modeled for a specific use case. This enables the lean representation of a business process. The projected behavior counterpart is created for the projection view—the *projection behavior*—in which the operations specific to the use case are included. Finally, a service is created, which consists of a service definition and a service binding. Entities are exposed through the service definition, which determines which entities are available in the service. Exposure of the entities takes place in the service definition; i.e., entities that are made available in the service are included in the service definition. Based on a service definition, the service binding allows the external use of the business object via OData V2/V4 or a Web API.
3. **Service consumption**—this layer is where the OData service is made available to various clients. It can serve as a UI service, which is used by SAP Fiori Elements applications, or as a Web API, which is accessible as a public interface and can be connected by any OData client. The Web API provides the data without specific UI information in its metadata and is therefore suitable for consumption by clients.

The three-tier architecture in the RAP enables a clear division of responsibilities, optimizes the development process, and promotes the creation of scalable and maintainable OData services that are specifically tailored to optimization for SAP HANA.

3.2 Business objects

3.2.1 General principles

In the context of RAP, business objects (BOs) are real enterprise application artifacts that represent a specific business entity. A purchase order (PO) or a sales order (SO) in SAP are perfect examples of BOs in RAP. They represent important components of an application and contain structured information about the corresponding business processes.

With the help of Figure 3.2, we would like to explain the rough structure of a BO.

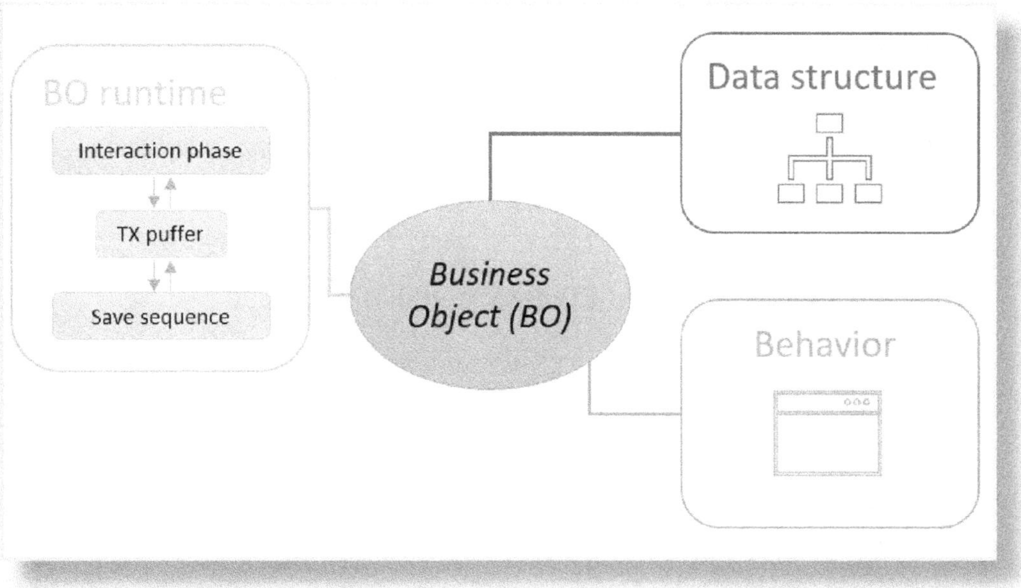

Figure 3.2: Business Object—structure

A business object has three characteristics:

1. **Data structure**—the structure of a BO is defined by the relational connections in a tree structure. In the flight reference model, for example, various entities such as flights, passengers and flight bookings can be linked to provide a comprehensive picture of flight data. In the ABAP environment, these structures are modeled using CDS entities, which provide a clear, easy-to-understand, and maintainable basis for the data model.

2. **Behavior**—BOs also have defined behavior. In general, this includes all basic and application-specific operations (CRUD, actions, functions) that are relevant for the application's business logic. ETags, authorizations, feature controls and drafting functionality are also defined in the behavior. The behavior of a BO is used for the seamless integration of business logic and data modeling. Behaviors are described in more detail in Section 3.3.

3. **BO runtime**—during runtime, a BO passes through the BO runtime. Various operations are applied to the object in this phase. Changes are stored temporarily in a transactional buffer (TX buffer) in order to process several operations efficiently. Only at the end of a transaction is the data permanently saved to the database in a defined sequence *(save sequence)*.

The use of BO in RAP enables developers to create robust and extensible enterprise applications. Clear structuring of data in BO, separation of business logic and data modeling, and efficient processing of operations all contribute to the development of high-quality applications. In combination with the RAP model, this ensures modern and database-supported development of enterprise applications in the SAP ABAP environment.

3.2.2 Creating the flight BO data model

In this section, we will create the BO data model using the flight reference model, which will provide the basis for our developments.

The first step is to create a new package, *ZRAP_FLIGHT*, in which we will carry out our further developments. To do this, right-click on the system and select NEW ❶ and ABAP PACKAGE ❷, as shown in Figure 3.3.

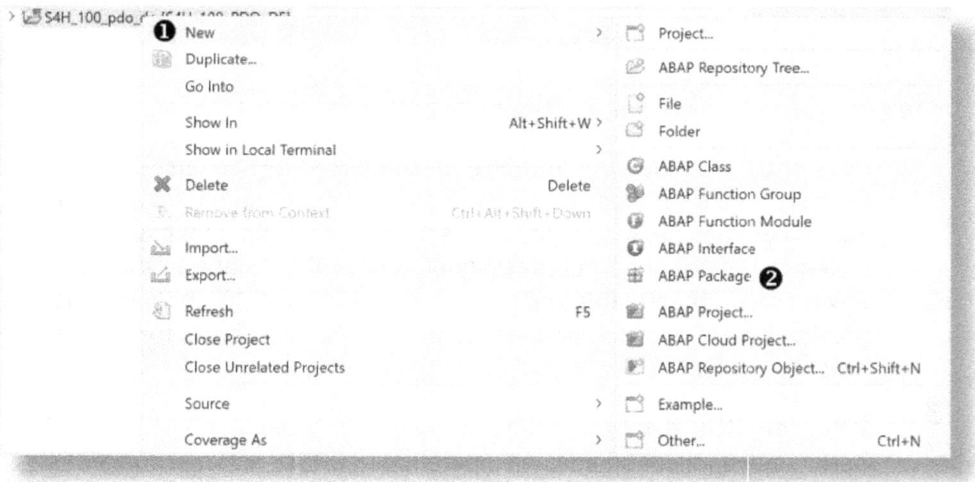

Figure 3.3: Creating new ABAP package (step 1)

In the creation dialog box (see Figure 3.4), we assign the NAME *ZRAP_FLIGHT* ❶ and the DESCRIPTION *RAP Flight Model* ❷. This is confirmed by clicking on the NEXT button ❸.

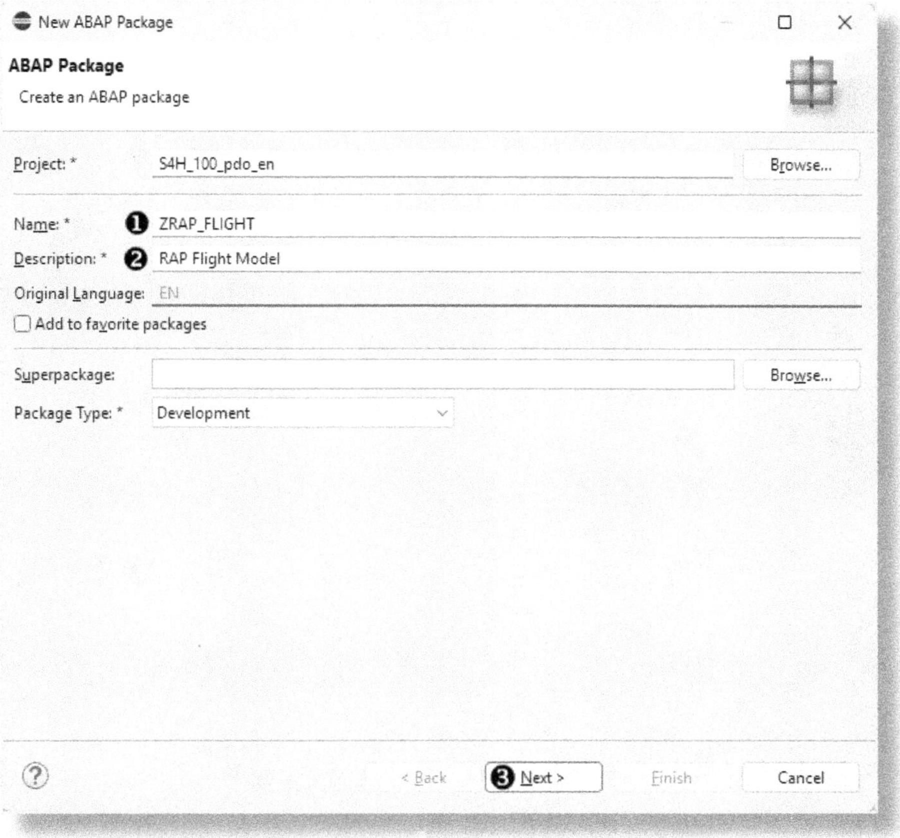

Figure 3.4: Creating new ABAP package (step 2)

In the next step, we select the *HOME* ❶ software component and confirm by clicking on NEXT ❷, as shown in Figure 3.5.

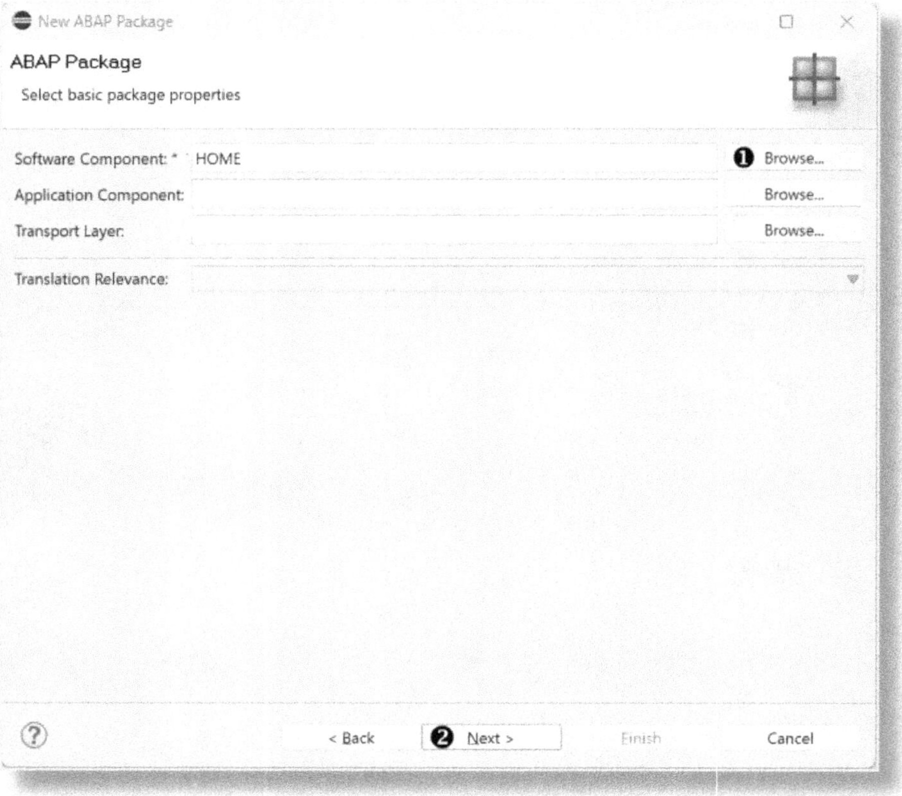

Figure 3.5: Creating new ABAP package (step 3)

Before the package can be created, we have to select an existing TRANSPORT REQUEST ❶ or CREATE A NEW REQUEST ❷, as shown in Figure 3.6. We then create the package by clicking on the FINISH button ❸.

Adding a package to favorites

You can add the created package to your favorites in Eclipse, which will help you find it more quickly in future. To do this, right-click on FAVORITE PACKAGES and select ADD PACKAGE in the context menu. To search for the package, enter the package name *ZRAP_FLIGHT*.

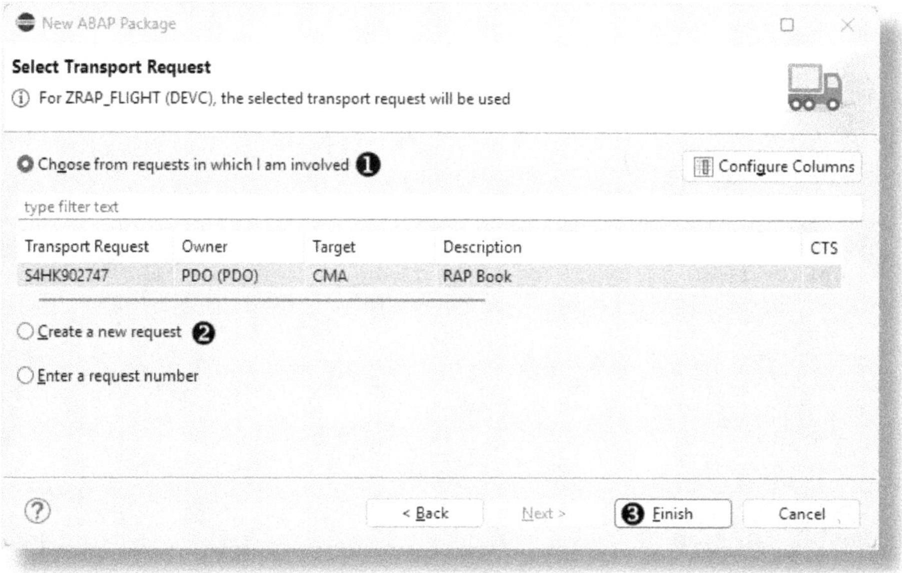

Figure 3.6: Selecting transport request

After the ZRAP_FLIGHT package has been opened in Eclipse, we can create a new CDS view. Right-click on the package and select the menu item NEW ❶, and then click on option OTHER ABAP REPOSITORY OBJECT ❷ (see Figure 3.7).

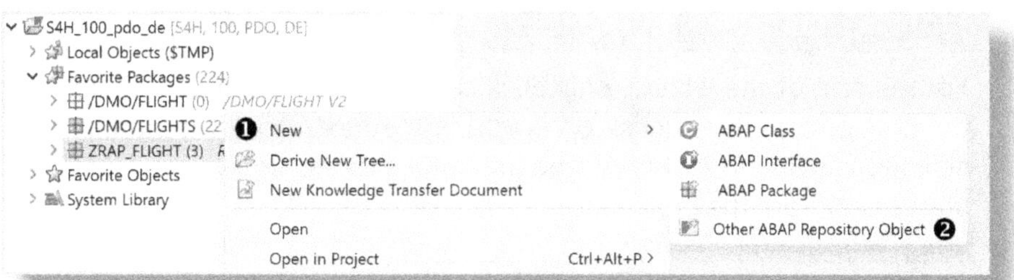

Figure 3.7: Creating new ABAP repository object

In the creation dialog box (see Figure 3.8), the DATA DEFINITION ❶ type is accessed by using the search function and entering the partial term *Data De*. Select DATA DEFINITION and confirm by clicking on the NEXT button ❷.

Figure 3.8: Creating data definition

In the next step, we assign the NAME *Z_I_TRAVEL* ❶ and a DESCRIPTION ❷, and confirm the entries by clicking on NEXT ❸, as shown in Figure 3.9.

! Always confirm with "Next"

For the rest of the wizard, only click on the NEXT button until FINISH is the only option. If you click on FINISH in the next step of the transport selection, an incorrect entity type might be created, and you will have to start again from the beginning.

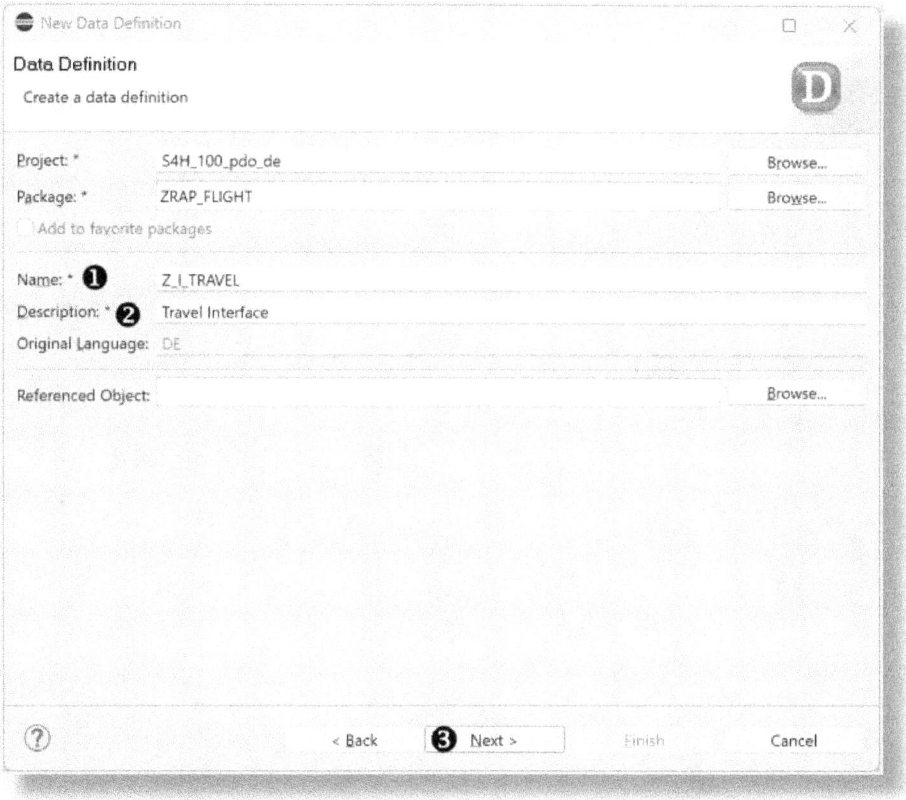

Figure 3.9: New data definition

Once the transport has been determined, we reach the Templates selection (see Figure 3.10). Select the template Define Root View Entity ❶ and confirm the selection by clicking on Finish ❷.

Figure 3.10: Selecting root view entity template

An *interface view* with the name *Z_I_TRAVEL* has now been created. This interface view acts as an interface to retrieve and manage data from the underlying database table. We now need to make changes to the generated view so that it is based on the database table */DMO/TRAVEL*.

The interface view *Z_I_TRAVEL* should contain specific fields from the table; these are important for our application logic. When designing the interface view, it is crucial to carefully select which fields are to be presented in the application and in the service.

In the source code example in Listing 3.1, you can see the CDS syntax for the new interface view.

```
@AccessControl.authorizationCheck: #NOT_REQUIRED
@EndUserText.label: 'Travel Interface'
define root view entity Z_I_TRAVEL
as select from /dmo/travel
{
 key travel_id as TravelId,
 agency_id as AgencyId,
 customer_id as CustomerId,
 begin_date as BeginDate,
 end_date as EndDate,
 booking_fee as BookingFee,
 total_price as TotalPrice,
 currency_code as CurrencyCode,
 description as Description,
 status as Status,
 createdby as Createdby,
 createdat as Createdat,
 lastchangedby as Lastchangedby,
 lastchangedat as Lastchangedat
}
```

Listing 3.1: Interface view "Z_I_TRAVEL"

☛ CDS view entity versus DDIC-based CDS view

In this book, we have used the concept of the *view entity* or *root view entity*. It is important to understand how this differs from the conventional DDIC-based CDS view. The CDS view entity is the successor to the classic DDIC-based CDS view and is characterized by subtle improvements and extended functionalities.

We now create a second CDS view with the name *Z_C_TRAVEL*—the projection view. This is a projected view of the previously created interface view *Z_I_TRAVEL*. This enables us to display data that is specifically filtered, harmonized and specified for special requirements without changing the basic data structure. This also creates a more flexible and customized presentation of the data for specific use cases. In the next step, we assign the NAME *Z_C_TRAVEL* ❶ and the DESCRIPTION *Travel Projection View* ❷ and confirm the entries by clicking on the NEXT button ❸, as shown in Figure 3.11.

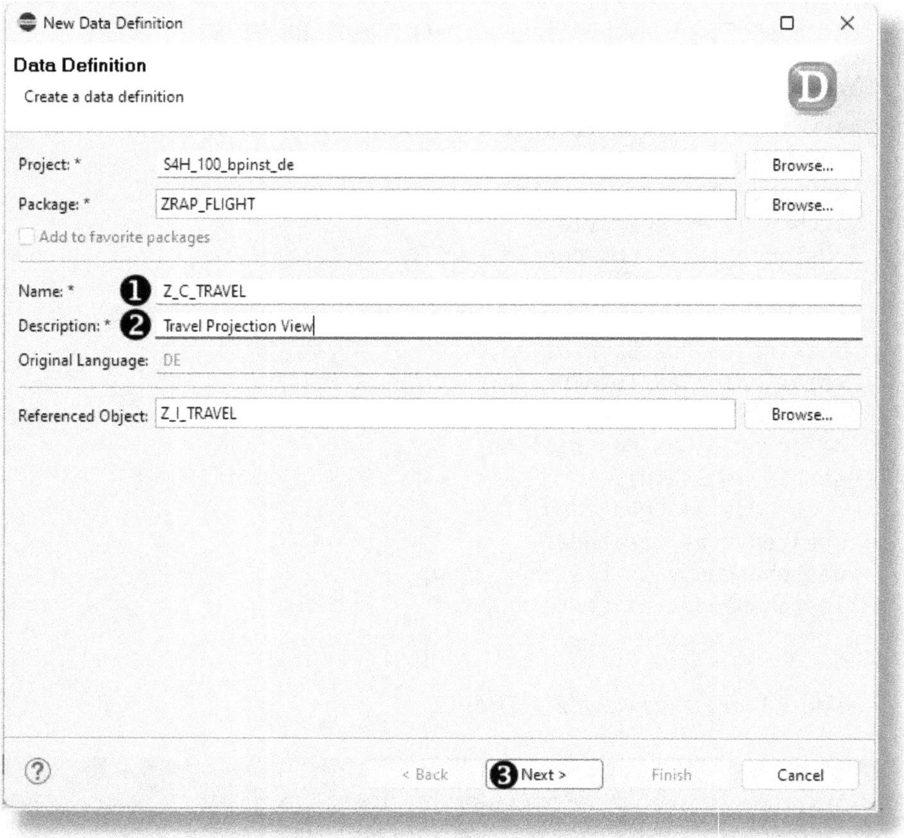

Figure 3.11: Creating projection view "Z_C_TRAVEL"

When choosing a template, we select Define Projection View ❶ and confirm the selection by clicking on Finish ❷, as shown in Figure 3.12.

Figure 3.12: Projection view—selecting a template

In the source code example in Listing 3.2, we can see the CDS syntax for the new projection view.

```
@AccessControl.authorizationCheck: #NOT_REQUIRED
@EndUserText.label: 'Travel Projection View'
define root view entity Z_C_TRAVEL
  provider contract transactional_query
  as projection on Z_I_TRAVEL
{
  @UI.facet: [ {
    id: 'idIdentification',
    type: #IDENTIFICATION_REFERENCE,
    label: 'Travel',
    position: 10
  } ]
```

```
  @UI: { lineItem: [{ position: 10 }],
         identification: [{ position: 10 }],
         selectionField: [{ position: 10 }] }
  key TravelId,
  @UI: { lineItem: [{ position: 20 }],
         identification: [{ position: 20 }] }
  AgencyId,
  @UI: { lineItem: [{ position: 30 }],
         identification: [{ position: 30 }],
         selectionField: [{ position: 20 }] }
  CustomerId,
  @UI: { lineItem: [{ position: 40 }],
         identification: [{ position: 40 }] }
  BeginDate,
  @UI: { lineItem: [{ position: 50 }],
         identification: [{ position: 50 }] }
  EndDate,
  @UI: { lineItem: [{ position: 60 }],
         identification: [{ position: 60 }] }
  BookingFee,
  @UI: { lineItem: [{ position: 70 }],
         identification: [{ position: 70 }] }
  TotalPrice,
  @UI: { lineItem: [{ position: 80 }],
         identification: [{ position: 80 }] }
  CurrencyCode,
  @UI: { lineItem: [{ position: 90 }],
         identification: [{ position: 90 }] }
  Description,
  @UI: { lineItem: [{ position: 100 }],
         identification: [{ position: 100 }] }
  Status,
  Createdby,
  Createdat,
  Lastchangedby,
  Lastchangedat
}
```

Listing 3.2: Projection view "Z_C_TRAVEL"

In the example, we have included all the interface view fields in the projection view. In theory, it is possible to include a subset of the fields, depending on what is needed for the application. Finally, activate the projection view *Z_C_TRAVEL* by clicking on the button.

Annotations can be defined in the CDS environment. In our example, we have done this directly in the projection view. We would like to point out here that we assume our readers have a basic knowledge of CDS annotations.

Further information on CDS

For further information on the topic of CDS, refer to the book "Practical Guide to SAP Core Data Services[1]", by Deepa Rawat.

Subscribers to Espresso Tutorials' SAP Learning Platform (et.training) can also watch the video "CDS Views in S/4HANA Analytics – Making Friends", by Dimitry Kuznetsov, which can be found at: *https://et.training/dashboard/product/video/780.*

3.3 Behavior—definition and implementation

3.3.1 General principles

The definition and implementation of a *behavior* in a business object (BO) can be metaphorically likened to the principles of the behavioral psychology of dogs. Similar to the way a dog reacts to certain stimuli through training and conditioning, so too are possible actions or behaviors defined, which can then be applied to a BO.

Defining behavior

In dog behavioral psychology, behavior is specifically defined for particular situations. For example, a dog can learn to sit on the command "Sit!". This behavior is defined by clear instructions. Similarly, the behavior definition in the RAP model determines which actions and attributes can be applied to a BO. On one hand, the service supports basic CRUD operations (create, read, update, and delete) that perform the creation, reading, update and deletion of entries, as well as user-defined business-relevant actions. On the other hand, entity-specific attributes can be defined, such as ETag for data consistency, authorization for access permissions, feature control for dynamic

[1] Rawat, D. (2019). *Practical Guide to SAP Core Data Services*. Espresso Tutorials.

control of specific functions, or lock for managing data locks and drafting. The behavior definition is defined with *Behavior Definition Language (BDL)*. BDL is a newly introduced language in the RAP model and is similar to CDS.

Behavior implementation

Implementation of the defined behavior requires training and execution. A dog learns to respond to the sit command by repeatedly executing the instruction and being rewarded. In a BO, implementation of a behavior is carried out by an ABAP code. This code defines how the actions specified in the behavior definition are to be executed. For example, the implementation of an *approve* action can require approval by a superior and then a status change of a BO data record. Behavior implementation is performed using ABAP code in an ordinary ABAP class.

Parallels to behavioral psychology

Similar to the way a dog's behavior is shaped by consistent instructions and rewards, the definition and implementation of behavior in the RAP model enables the targeted control of possible actions on a BO. This promotes consistent and predictable system behavior, just like a trained animal that reacts predictably to certain stimuli. The analogy to behavioral psychology illustrates how precise behavior definition and implementation in a BO can enable smooth and targeted business logic.

3.3.2 Managed versus unmanaged behavior

In the context of behaviors, three primary behaviors are defined to specify the handling and management of data in RAP applications.

Managed behavior

Managed behavior is the standard mode in RAP development projects. In this mode, the RAP framework takes over the automated control of data management and validation. This means that CRUD operations are largely controlled by the SAP standard framework logic. The framework performs comprehensive input data checks (for accuracy and completeness), manages transactions to ensure data consistency, handles any errors that occur, and automatically controls authorizations for data access. The managed behavior approach should be the first choice in most cases, as it offers the most comprehensive functions and security mechanisms.

Managed with unmanaged save

Managed behavior also has the option *managed with unmanaged save*. This approach enables the combination of automated data management in managed mode, with the ability to independently control and optimize CRUD operations, especially for specific storage or performance requirements. However, the unmanaged save function should be used with caution because it involves greater developer responsibility for the save process. It should be considered only in special cases; for example, when an operation is processed across multiple database tables (i.e., when other tables need to be written during create, update or delete actions).

Unmanaged behavior

Unmanaged behavior should only be considered as a last resort. In this mode, developers are responsible for implementing CRUD operations, validations, transaction management and authorization checks themselves. This mode offers the highest level of customizability but should only be used if the requirements are exceptionally complex or special, and when the standard functionality of the RAP framework is not sufficient.

3.3.3 Behavior implementation for consumption view

In RAP, the behavior definition is tailored specifically to the data model used in the consumption view. This adapted behavior definition supplements its data and functions and forms a subset of the interface view's behavior definition. This means that the consumption view does not have its own behavior implementation; instead, it uses the interface view's behavior definition, which already defines all the necessary operations and functions.

While the behavior definition for the consumption view is projected and adapted, the behavior implementation, which executes all operations and functions, remains unchanged. The projected consumption view's behavior definition accesses the functions of the interface view's behavior implementation to provide the required actions and operations for the BO. This ensures efficient and targeted functionality in the consumption view without the need for separate implementation. This also facilitates development and ensures consistency of business logic across different views.

As an example, you might have an interface view that defines and implements the actions. The consumption view uses these definitions but does not have its own action implementation. Instead, it uses the action already defined and its implementation in the interface view.

3.3.4 Creating the behavior

In this section, we define and implement the behavior for the previously created BO data model using the flight reference model.

First, we create a new behavior definition for the interface view of the travel data model (*Z_I_TRAVEL*). To do this, right-click on the CDS view Z_I_TRAVEL and select the menu item NEW BEHAVIOR DEFINITION (see Figure 3.13).

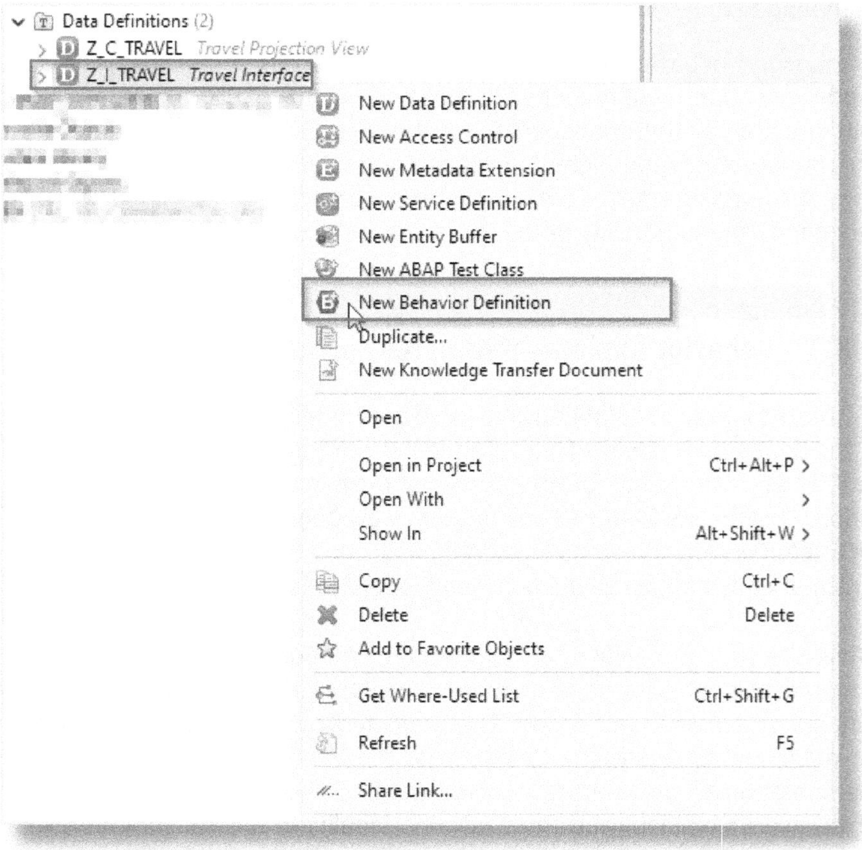

Figure 3.13: Creating a new behavior definition

In the creation dialog box, as shown in Figure 3.14, we assign the DESCRIPTION *Travel Interface Behavior Definition* ❶ and IMPLEMENTATION TYPE *Managed* ❷. We confirm the selection by clicking on NEXT ❸.

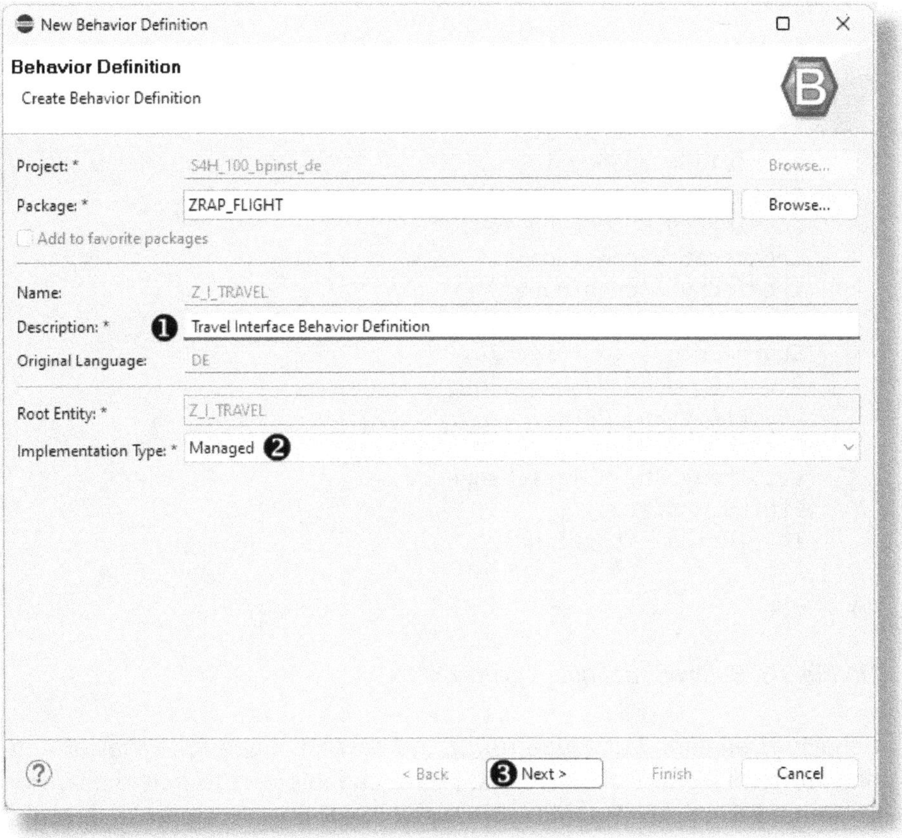

Figure 3.14: Creating a behavior definition—dialog box

Listing 3.3 shows the BDL syntax for the newly created behavior definition *Z_I_TRAVEL*. We have adapted the name of the class to *ZCL_I_TRAVEL* for conformity. In addition, we have added a mapping for the assignment of the database fields to the entity fields.

```
managed implementation in class zcl_i_travel unique;
strict;
define behavior for Z_I_TRAVEL //alias <alias_name>
persistent table /DMO/TRAVEL
lock master
authorization master ( instance )
//etag master <field_name>
```

```
{
  create;
  update;
  delete;

  mapping for /dmo/travel
  {
    TravelId = travel_id;
    AgencyId = agency_id;
    BeginDate = begin_date;
    BookingFee = booking_fee;
    Createdat = createdat;
    Createdby = createdby;
    CurrencyCode = currency_code;
    CustomerId = customer_id;
    Description = description;
    EndDate = end_date;
    Lastchangedat = lastchangedat;
    Lastchangedby = lastchangedby;
    Status = status;
    TotalPrice = total_price;
  }
}
```

Listing 3.3: Behavior definition syntax

Behavior Definition Language (BDL), the new language for behavior definitions, provides a declarative and more readable way to define behavior, unlike traditional ABAP syntax. BDL uses JSON-like structures to describe the behavior.

To explain this, let's take a closer look at the syntax of the generated behavior definition:

- `managed implementation in class zcl_i_travel unique;`—indicates that the behavior is implemented in the ABAP class *zcl_i_travel*. The `unique` keyword means that only one instance of this class is permitted.
- `Strict;`—strict mode ensures that the BO follows best practice and is both lifecycle-stable and upgrade-safe. The `strict` or `strict(2)` code components enforce stricter rules and syntax checks to ensure that only specifically declared operations and fields are used.

It is recommended to always use the latest version of strict mode to ensure the strictest checks and best practices.

- `define behavior for Z_I_TRAVEL`—behavior for the *Z_I_TRAVEL* interface is defined here.
- `persistent table /DMO/TRAVEL`—specifies which database table will be the basis for the interface. In this case, it is database table */DMO/TRAVEL*.
- `lock master`—specifies that locks are used at the master data level. This means that the locks are managed at the level of all data records in the table.
- `authorization master (instance)`—defines the type of authorization check. In this case, an authorization check is performed at an instance level; i.e. the authorizations for access to a specific data record instance are checked.
- `create; update; delete;`—the operations that are permitted in the context of the managed model are defined here. The framework then handles the corresponding processing based on the standard rules and the specific implementation of the managed model.
- `mapping for /DMO/TRAVEL`–defines how the BO fields (*Z_I_TRAVEL*) are mapped to those of the database table (*/DMO/TRAVEL*). Each assignment (e.g. `TravelId = travel_id;`) specifies that the field in the BO (e.g. `TravelId`) corresponds to the data in the corresponding table field (here `travel_id`). This is essential for data integrity and correct data manipulation in the managed scenario.

We now have a ready-made basic behavior definition that describes the behaviors of the *Z_I_TRAVEL* data model. Next, we need to create the corresponding behavior implementation. To do this, either left-click on the quick fix button ( ) in the first line of the behavior definition ❶ (see Figure 3.15), or open the quick fix window by pressing the `Ctrl` + `1` keys. Double-click on CREATE BEHAVIOR IMPLEMENTATION CLASS ZCL_I_TRAVEL ❷.

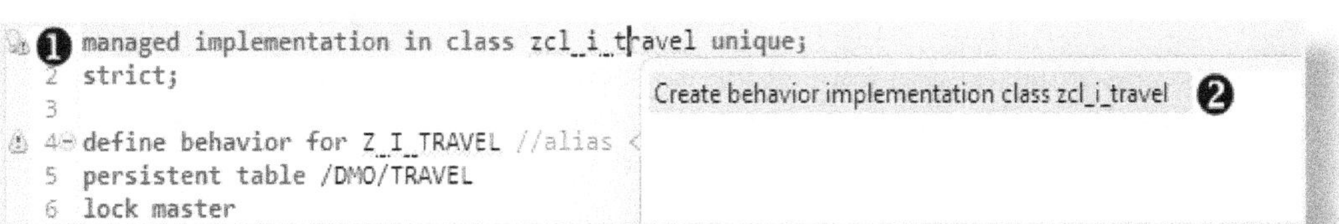

Figure 3.15: Creating behavior implementation

In the window shown in Figure 3.16, we have the option of specifying our own DESCRIPTION for the class ❶. We then confirm our entries by clicking on NEXT ❷.

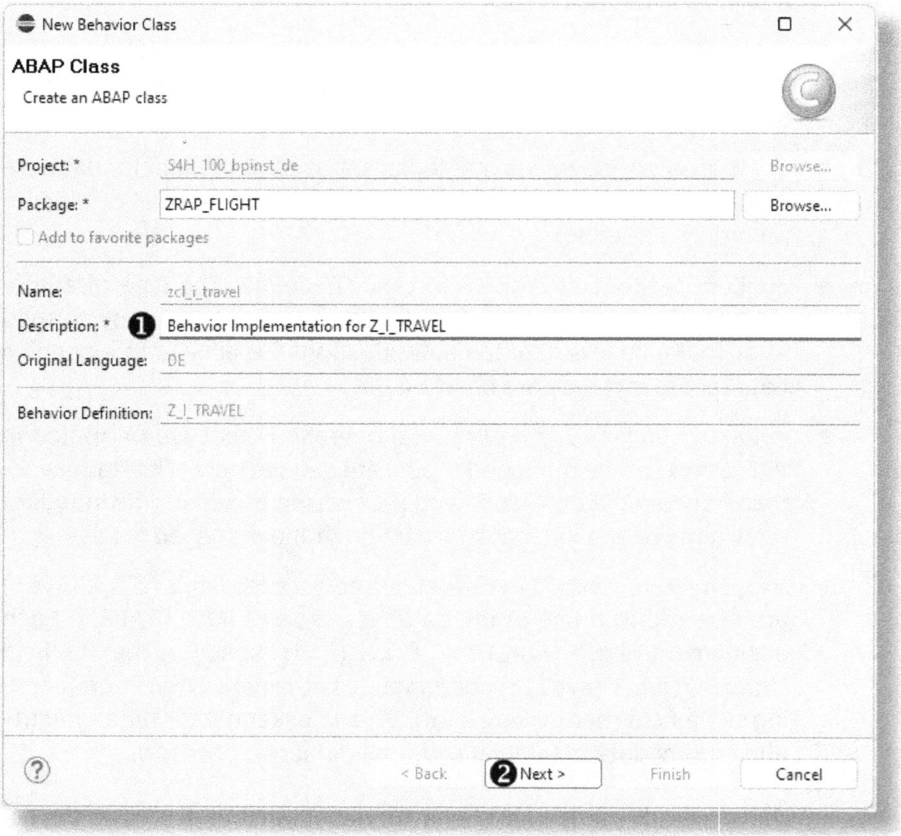

Figure 3.16: Creating class "Behavior Implementation"

We are taken to the next screen where we might need to specify a transport, and we complete the installation by clicking on FINISH.

A notable feature of the BEHAVIOR IMPLEMENTATION class is that it often does not contain a lot of code at the top level. Instead, much of the specific functionality and logic is implemented through local classes within the implementation. This results in the following advantages:

- **Structured organization**—the use of local classes within the BEHAVIOR IMPLEMENTATION class enables a clearly structured and modular organization of the code. Each local class can be responsible for specific aspects of BO behavior, such as validation, calculations or special business logic.

- **Maintainability and readability**—this separation makes the main class clearer and easier to maintain. The actual implementation of the various operations and business logic is encapsulated in the associated local classes, which improves the readability and maintainability of the code.
- **Focus on delegation and encapsulation**—the main class acts more as a coordinator/delegator that forwards the relevant tasks to the responsible local classes. This structure promotes the encapsulation and reusability of code, because local classes can perform specific tasks independently and in isolation from other parts of the application.

Various subclasses are used in ABAP behavior definition classes; in a regular scenario, it is only one global class. In addition to global classes, there are also local classes. Traditionally, local classes were used less, and global classes were preferred for many applications. With RAP, however, local classes are gaining in importance. They encapsulate specific business logic and improve the structure and maintainability of business objects. The advantages of local classes are encapsulation, modularity, and flexibility.

We now navigate to the LOCAL TYPES tab (see Figure 3.17) and note that only the *get_instance_authorizations* method has been generated—this is used for the authorization check of instances in connection with the RAP implementation.

Figure 3.17: "Local Types" tab

The *create*, *update* and *delete* methods have not been generated, because we defined the implementation as a managed model.

We have also created the behavior components for the *Z_I_TRAVEL* interface view. Finally, we need to create the behavior definition for the projected data model. To do this, we right-click on the CDS view Z_C_TRAVEL ❶ and select menu item NEW BEHAVIOR DEFINITION ❷ (see Figure 3.18).

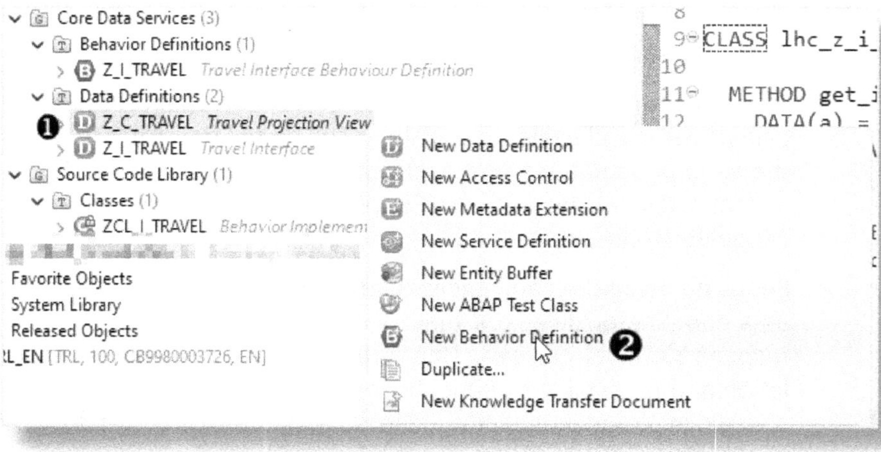

Figure 3.18: Creating behavior definition (projection)—dialog box

In the subsequent window (see Figure 3.19) we enter the Description *Travel Projection View* ❶. We then confirm our entries by clicking on Next ❷.

Figure 3.19: Behavior Implementation (Projection)—creation dialog

We are then taken to the next screen, where we may have to specify a transport, and we complete the installation by clicking on FINISH.

In Listing 3.4, we can see that the syntax for the behavior definition projection might take some getting used to.

```
projection;
strict;

define behavior for Z_C_TRAVEL //alias <alias_name>
{
  use create;
  use update;
  use delete;
}
```

Listing 3.4: Behavior definition—projection

In the first line, the keyword `projection` is used to indicate that this is a projected behavior definition. In the `define behavior` clause, the operations that are required in this specific case are added to the projection with command `use`.

From an architectural point of view, it is not necessary to create a separate behavior implementation for the projected view. Instead, the projected view's behavior definition uses the interface view's behavior implementation. The projection view's behavior definition is a subset of the operations defined in the interface view. This means that we use the implementation that was provided in the interface view.

Simply put, when we define the behavior for a projected view, we do not have to create a completely new implementation logic. The behavior definition for the projected view essentially says that we use the rules and operations already defined in the interface view. This is possible because the operations defined in the projection are a subset of what has already been defined in the broader interface view. It is a way to reuse the implementation logic from the interface view for the specific projected view case.

3.4 Business services

In this section, we delve into the world of services. *Services* are central components of RAP and offer a structured way of organizing business logic and data access.

Business services in RAP are RESTful services that can be called by a consumer. Their essence lies in the exposure of the data model with the associated behavioral logic. A complete business service consists of a service definition and a service binding. The business service is the end product of RAP. This section highlights the concepts of service definition and service binding, which are fundamental to the delivery of business services. We will now examine how these concepts help orchestrate the interaction between the user interface and the underlying data.

3.4.1 General principles

Service definition

The *service definition* plays a crucial role in RAP. The key concepts are as follows:

- **Purpose**—the service definition describes which entities are to be released to enable a specific RESTful service.
- **ABAP repository object**—as an ABAP repository object, the service definition can be managed in Eclipse and provides access to important functions such as transport and syntax checks.
- **Protocol-independent and application-oriented**—protocol-independent means that the service definition is not fixed to a specific communication protocol. It focuses on which data should be released for a specific application.
- **Generic derivation**—the service definition is comparable to an abstract blueprint based on the data model. It describes how the data is organized and provided, without going into technical details.

The service definition in RAP (see Listing 3.5) follows a clear structure.

```
DEFINE SERVICE ServiceDefinitionName
{
  EXPOSE Entity1 AS Alias1;
  EXPOSE Entity2 AS Alias2;
  EXPOSE ...;
  EXPOSE EntityN as AliasN;
}
```

Listing 3.5: Service definition—general

Starting with the keywords `DEFINE SERVICE`, the context and name of the service are defined, followed by curly brackets that enclose the definition area. Within these brackets, the data entities to be released (name of the CDS view) are specified with the keyword `EXPOSE`, whereby alias names can optionally be used. This service definition serves as an architectural blueprint and forms the basis for the configuration of the actual service binding. It enables precise control over which data is available for external access.

Service binding

A *service binding* is an object in the ABAP repository that is used to bind a service definition to a client-server communication protocol such as OData.

The service binding is based directly on a service definition that is derived from the underlying CDS data model. Multiple service bindings can be based on a single service definition. The separation between service definition and service binding makes it possible to integrate a service into different service protocols without the need for a new implementation. Services implemented in this way are based on a separation of the service protocol from the actual business logic.

When creating the service binding, two fundamental properties need to be considered—the HTTP protocol and the scenario.

HTTP protocol

- **OData V2**—version 2 of the Open Data Protocol. It enables the exchange of data via HTTP in a standardized format and is often used for the integration of applications.

- **OData V4**—the latest version of the Open Data Protocol, offering extended functionality for transactional services compared to V2. It is therefore recommended for modern applications.
- **InA (Analytical Service)**—InA stands for *Information Access* and is an SAP-proprietary protocol. This protocol is used specifically for analytical services that are released for user interfaces. It enables access to analytical information and is tailored to the needs of UI applications.

Scenario

- **Web API**—this scenario refers to the exposure of the service as a web API so that the service can be consumed by different applications or endpoints via the standardized OData protocol. It is suitable for situations in which the service is to be used by unknown users.
- **UI service**—a particularly suitable scenario for user interfaces. It is often used for SAP Fiori Elements and other UI clients and is designed to seamlessly integrate the service into user interfaces and ensure an optimized user experience.

Publishing a service binding means publishing the local service endpoint of an OData service. This is done via the Publish button in Eclipse. When the service publishing process is initiated, it triggers several processes that make the service available for use.

3.4.2 Service definition

In this section, we will create the service definition for our previously created data model. This forms the basis for the service binding.

First, right-click on our package ❶, select menu item New ❷, and then Other ABAP Repository Object ❸, as shown in Figure 3.20.

The New ABAP Repository Object dialog box then opens (see Figure 3.21).

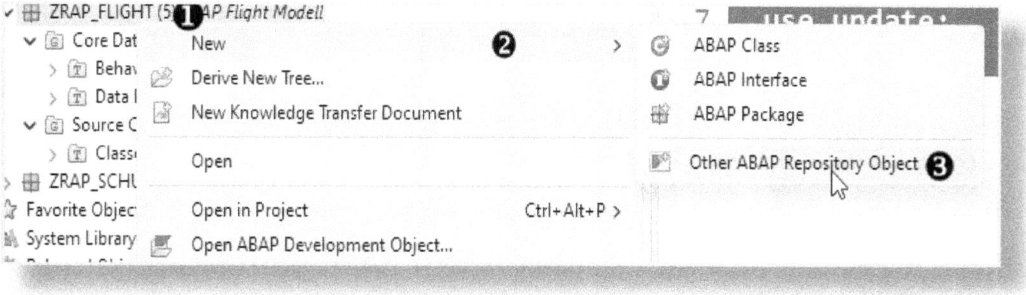

Figure 3.20: Creating a service definition

Enter the search term *Service Def* ❶ in the search field. Select the node Service Definition ❷ in the results tree and then click on the Next button ❸.

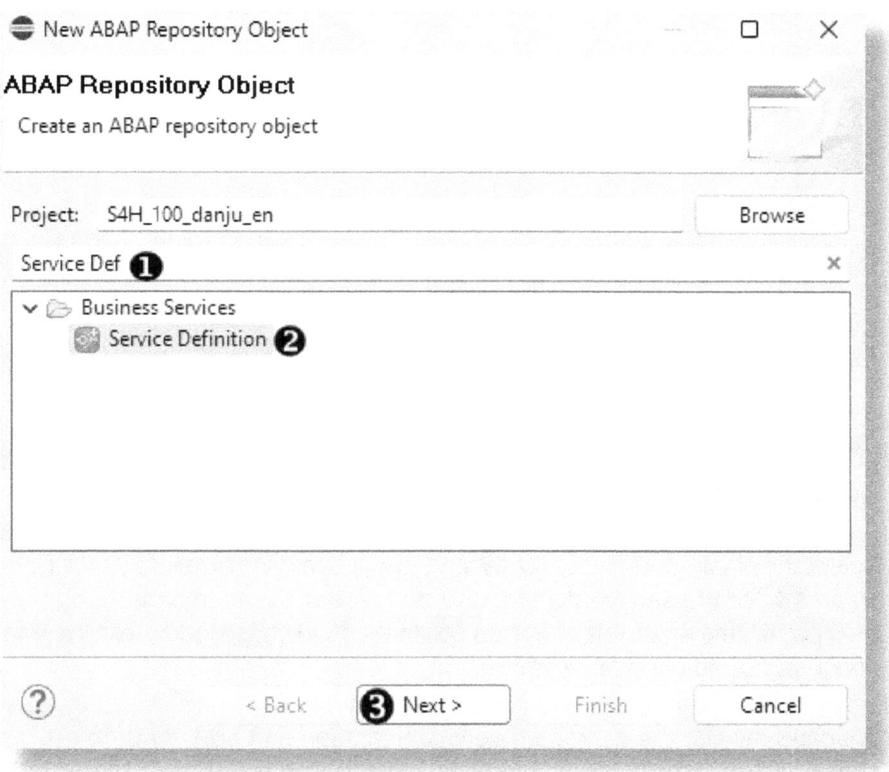

Figure 3.21: Service definition—dialog box 1

The resulting window is shown in Figure 3.22.

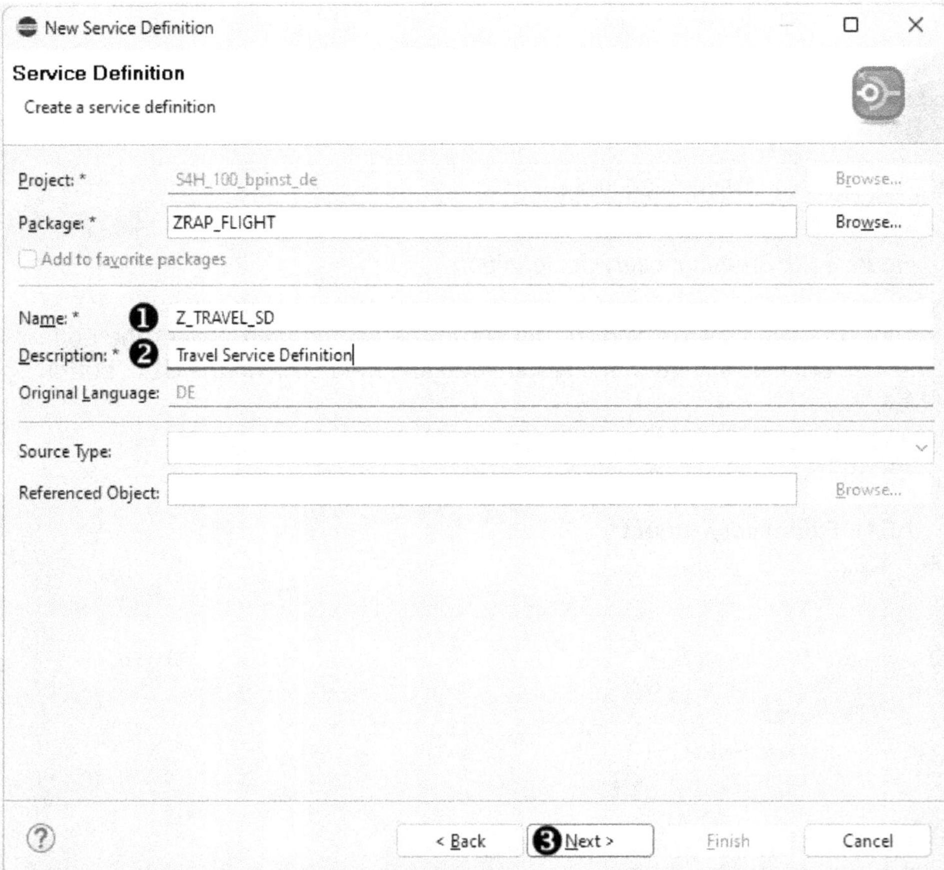

Figure 3.22: Service definition—dialog box 2

Select the NAME *Z_TRAVEL_SD* ❶ and the DESCRIPTION *Travel Service Definition* ❷ for the service definition to be created. We then confirm our entries by clicking on the NEXT button ❸. In the following window, click on the FINISH button to complete the creation.

We can now see the generated service definition and note that the syntax check shows an error. We should still "expose" the previously created projection view in this service definition. In Listing 3.6 we see the service definition with the exposed CDS entity.

```
@EndUserText.label: 'Travel Service Definition'
define service Z_TRAVEL_SD
{
  expose Z_C_TRAVEL;

}
```

Listing 3.6: Service definition

3.4.3 Service binding

In this section, we will create the service binding for the previously created service definition. The service binding forms the end product of our RAP model.

To start this process, first right-click on the previously created service definition Z_TRAVEL_SD ❶ (see Figure 3.23). In the context menu that opens, select NEW SERVICE BINDING ❷.

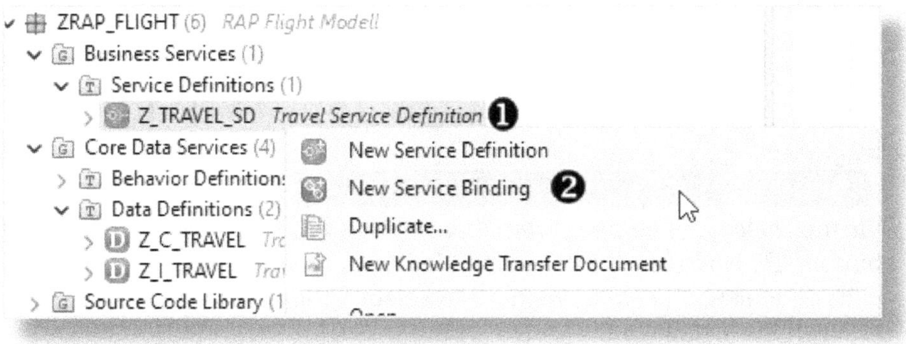

Figure 3.23: Creating service binding

In the following creation dialog box, we assign the NAME *Z_TRAVEL_SB_V2* ❶ and the DESCRIPTION *Travel Service Binding OData V2* ❷ (see Figure 3.24).

Figure 3.24: Creating service binding—dialog box

We then select the BINDING TYPE *OData V2 – UI* ❸. Finally, click on the NEXT button ❹. However, if the service binding is created in a local package, click on FINISH; otherwise, we have to select a transport in the next screen to finish the installation.

After populating the fields in the creation dialog box, the object opens in Eclipse (see Figure 3.25), where we first need to activate it.

To activate it, click on the button ❶, and then click on PUBLISH ❷ to publish the service.

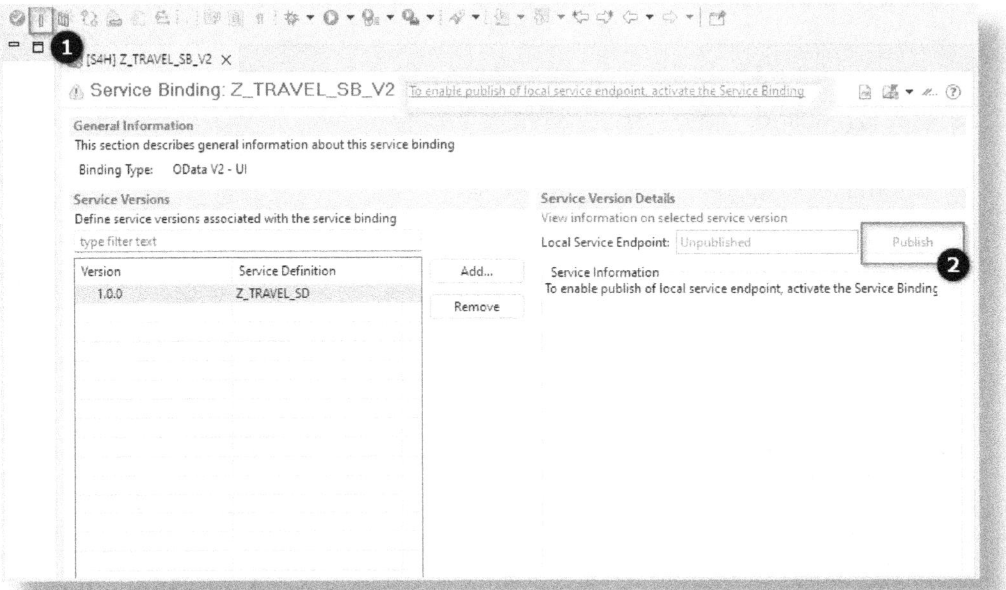

Figure 3.25: Publishing the service binding

During the publishing process, the service is automatically created in the background and assigned to the corresponding package. At the same time, the ICF node is activated, which makes the service accessible for external calls. The steps that were previously carried out when creating services using the *SEGW transaction* are now executed automatically during the publishing process. This means that the service is seamlessly integrated into the existing system without the need for additional manual intervention. This automation process optimizes the workflow and ensures that the service is delivered efficiently and reliably to external applications.

However, it is important to note that the process described only applies to system configurations where the frontend server is integrated into the same system, as is the case in an embedded hub scenario. In environments where a separate gateway system is used, you need to take additional steps. For version 2 OData services, the service must be activated in the gateway system using transaction */IWFND/MAINT_SERVICE*.

> **☛ OData—version 4**
>
> For version 4 OData services, activation in transaction */IWFND/V4_ADMIN* is required. These additional steps ensure that the service is configured correctly in the gateway system and made available for access by external applications.

3.4.4 Service consumption

Once the service binding has been successfully created, activated and published, the service can be displayed using the PREVIEW button ❶, as shown in Figure 3.26.

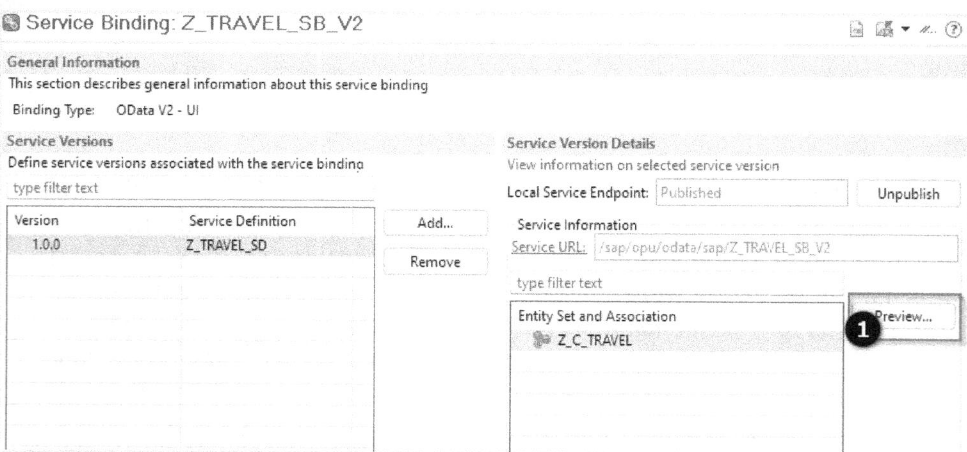

Figure 3.26: Service—Preview

A Fiori element list report application is generated based on the service. In the list report (see Figure 3.27) we can see all the UI-annotated fields, including the operations activated in the behavior definition. These appear as buttons in Fiori, excluding the update operation, because "Edit" would not make sense as a button without selecting a specific travel.

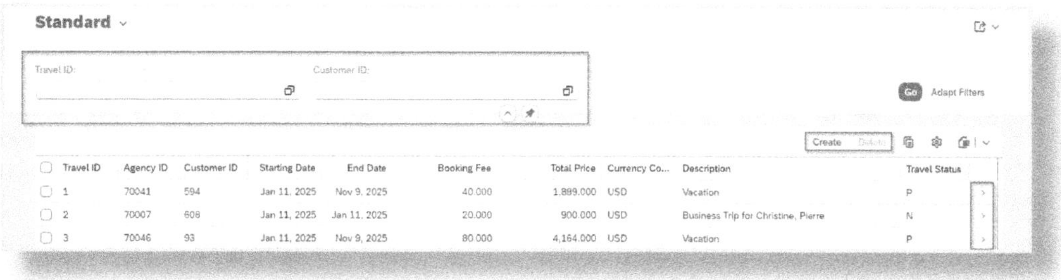

Figure 3.27: Fiori preview list

We can create a new entity via the CREATE button. Clicking on this button leads to an initial object page on which we fill in the entity data to be created. This new entity can then be displayed in the list.

Update and delete operations are instance-based or entity-based; i.e., an existing entity must be selected to initiate the update or delete operations. In this case, the latter can be carried out directly in the list report by selecting a specific row and clicking on the DELETE button. To update an entity, we navigate to the object entity page by clicking on the line item. Update and delete operations are carried out there (see Figure 3.28).

Figure 3.28: Fiori preview—object page

3.5 Conclusion

In this chapter, we explored the basic concepts of RAP. We introduced the model and provided a solid understanding of the central role of business objects (BOs). Furthermore, we looked in detail at the definition and implementation of behaviors and delved into the importance of business services. We also focused on creating a comprehensive RAP model that integrates and practically implements all these concepts.

Figure 3.29 provides an overview of all the components created in this chapter.

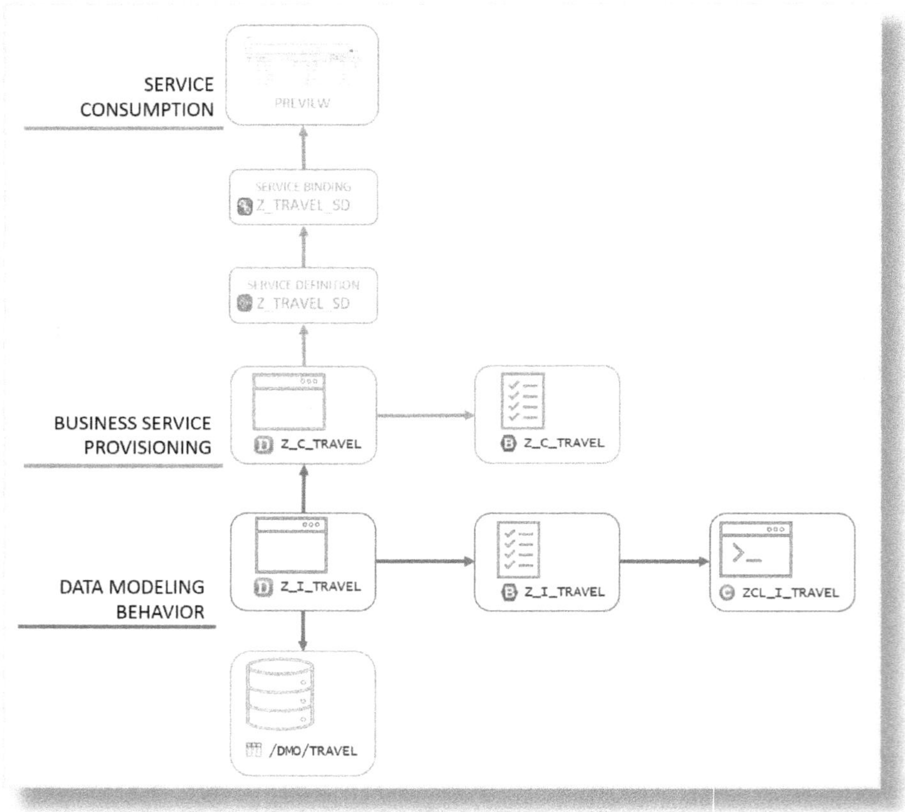

Figure 3.29: Overview of components created

These essential building blocks form the foundation for the development of efficient and scalable RESTful applications in the ABAP environment. Understanding these key concepts enables developers to design robust and flexibly extensible applications. In the next chapters, we will gain a more detailed insight into these concepts and discuss their implementation in real-life scenarios.

4 Entity Manipulation Language

In the previous chapter, we built the "travel" RAP model, from the definition of data structures to the provision of a RESTful service. This model serves as a solid foundation for us to now dive deeper into the new ABAP appendix of Entity Manipulation Language (EML).

Before we start with the methodologies in RAP, we would like to introduce the new ABAP language commands that have been introduced with the RAP model. In the previous chapters, we covered how to use the RAP model in combination with a Fiori Elements frontend. Instead of using a web-based frontend, it is also possible to view the behavior definition as an interface. It can be called by an ABAP program code. The advantage of this is that you only need to write the coding for the business object (BO) once and it can be used both for applications and for CRUD operations in ABAP programs.

4.1 Use cases

One of the most important use cases of Entity Manipulation Language (EML) is accessing the transactional buffer. This process is illustrated in the diagram shown in Figure 4.1.

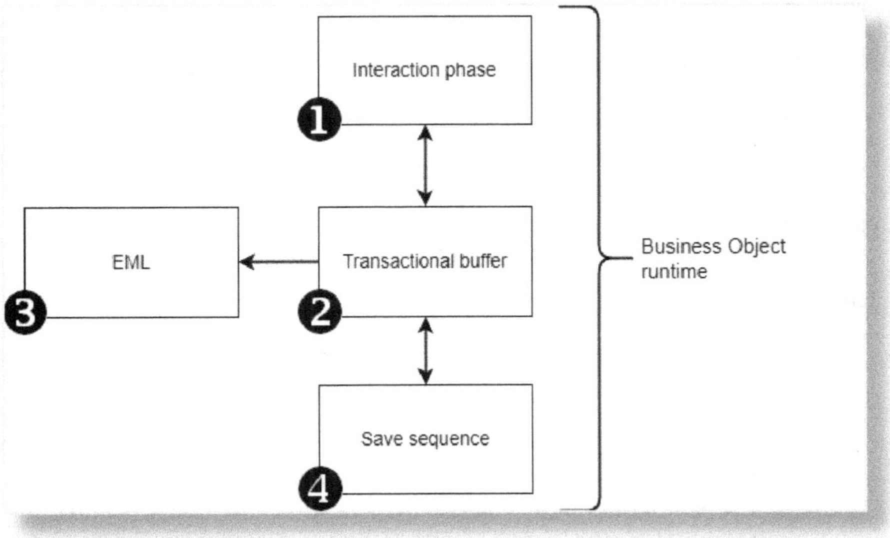

Figure 4.1: Use of EML within a BO

In the interaction phase ❶, the user makes entries; for example, in a web frontend. This input has not yet been persisted in the database and is therefore held in the transactional buffer ❷. EML ❸ is used so that ABAP can access the data that has not yet been saved. Before the data is saved with a unique key, a temporary key is generated for it. This identifies the new data record before the save sequence ❹ stores the data in the database.

As already mentioned, another use case is calling the BO's CRUD operations from an ABAP program. In addition, a comprehensive integration of BO is possible, whereby existing validations, actions, functions and CRUD operations can be reused. EML can also be used to write unit tests to ensure code quality.

4.2 Reading data (READ)

4.2.1 Syntax

The syntax for EML commands may seem unfamiliar at first, but it is logically structured and easy to interpret. To read data using EML, we use the ABAP language command `READ ENTITIES OF`. Let's look at how to read data using a specific example (see Listing 4.1).

```
READ ENTITIES OF z_c_travel
    ENTITY z_c_travel
    ALL FIELDS WITH VALUE #( ( TravelId = '$ID' ) )
    RESULT DATA(lt_travels)
    FAILED DATA(lt_failed)
    REPORTED DATA(lt_reported).
```

Listing 4.1: Syntax—"READ ENTITIES"

The lines in the syntax are as follows:

- `READ ENTITIES OF z_c_travel`—we call the ABAP statement `READ ENTITIES OF`, and then specify the behavior definition to be read, `Z_C_TRAVEL`.
- `ENTITY z_c_travel`—we specify the entity to be read, `Z_C_TRAVEL`. In a behavior definition, you can map various associations and compositions between entities, and it is also possible to assign alias names for entities. Therefore, at this point, you need to specifically

name the entity to be read from the behavior definition. In our example, the names of the behavior definition and the entity are identical.

- `ALL FIELDS WITH VALUE #((TravelId = '$ID'))`–we first define which fields we want to read. In this case, it is all of them, so we use the `ALL FIELDS` statement. We then use the `WITH` statement to pass a table containing the key fields of the entries to be read. In our specific example, we want to *read* the travel with the key `'$ID'`.
- We then have three tables:
  - `RESULT`–contains the successfully read data for the requested keys.
  - `FAILED`–if an entry cannot be read, the corresponding key is included in this table.
  - `REPORTED`–the returned messages are collected in this table.

4.2.2 Implementation

As a concrete example, we will now implement a method in a class that reads a travel and outputs the entry in the console in Eclipse.

We first create a new class with the name *ZCL_TRAVEL_SERVICE*. To do this, right-click on the source code library in the ZRAP_FLIGHT package and select menu item ABAP CLASS under NEW, as shown in Figure 4.2

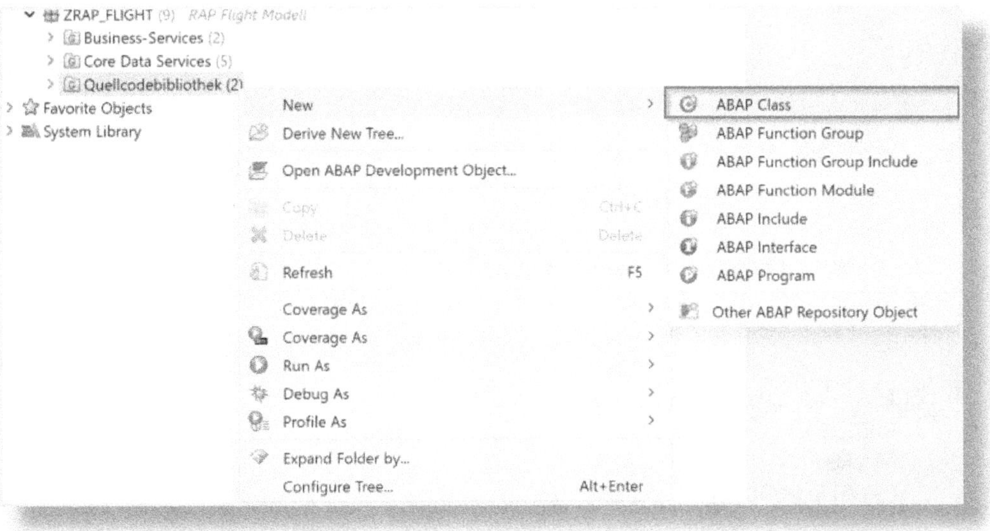

Figure 4.2: Creating a new class

In the next step (see Figure 4.3) we enter the NAME *ZCL_TRAVEL_SERVICE* as the class name ❶ and assign a DESCRIPTION ❷. We then add the interface *IF_OO_ADT_CLASSRUN* ❹ using the ADD button ❸. We confirm the entries by clicking on NEXT ❺. We then select a transport request and confirm by clicking on FINISH.

Figure 4.3: Creating a new class—ADT interface

The class has now been created but still has an empty implementation for the `if_oo_adt_classrun~main` method (see Listing 4.2). We will now implement this for the various CRUD operations.

```
CLASS zcl_travel_service DEFINITION
  PUBLIC
  FINAL
  CREATE PUBLIC .

  PUBLIC SECTION.
```

```
    METHODS constructor.
    DATA m_travel TYPE /dmo/travel_id.
    INTERFACES if_oo_adt_classrun.
  PROTECTED SECTION.
  PRIVATE SECTION.
ENDCLASS.



CLASS zcl_travel_service IMPLEMENTATION.
  METHOD constructor.
    SELECT SINGLE travel_id
      FROM /dmo/travel
      INTO @me->m_travel.
  ENDMETHOD.

  METHOD if_oo_adt_classrun~main.
  ENDMETHOD.

ENDCLASS.
```

Listing 4.2: Initial implementation

We extend the class by declaring the instance attribute *m_travel* (travel-ID) and implementing the constructor method. This method selects a random travel ID from the */DMO/TRAVEL* table and saves it in the instance attribute.

The example we looked at in Section 4.2.1 will now be partially adopted in our `main` method. In addition, we call the `write` method of the importing parameter to output the read data in the Eclipse console (see Listing 4.3).

```
  METHOD if_oo_adt_classrun~main.
    READ ENTITIES OF z_c_travel
      ENTITY z_c_travel
      ALL FIELDS WITH VALUE #( ( TravelId = me->m_travel ) )
      RESULT DATA(lt_travels)
      FAILED DATA(lt_failed)
      REPORTED DATA(lt_reported).

    out->write( data = lt_travels ).
  ENDMETHOD.
```

Listing 4.3: Implementing the "ZCL_TRAVEL_SERVICE" class

We now execute the class implementation by pressing function key [F9]—ABAP application (console). Alternatively, as shown in Figure 4.4, we can click on the execute button (▶). Select the line *ABAP Application (Console)* ❶ and confirm the selection by clicking on OK ❷.

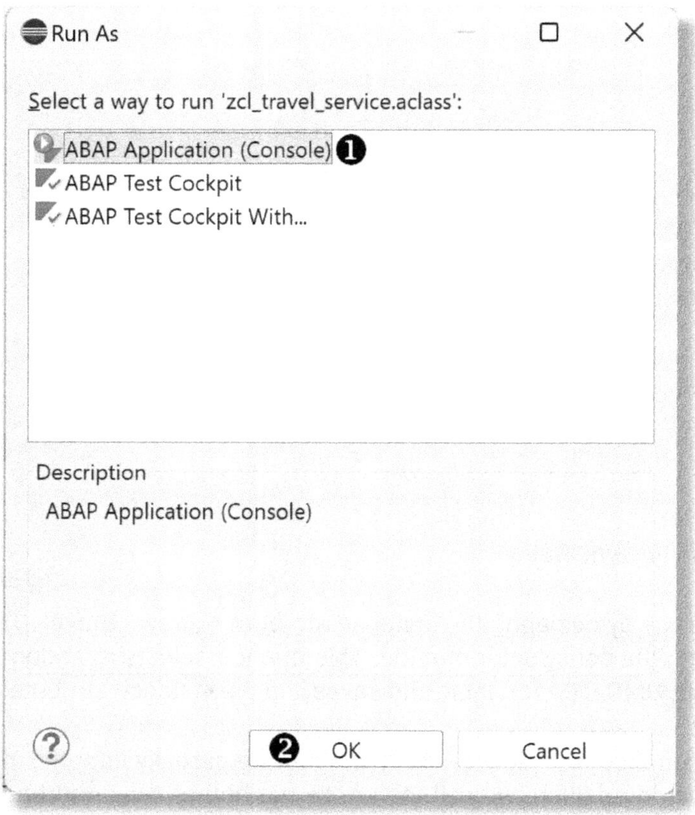

Figure 4.4: Running the application

After execution, the read travel values are displayed in the Eclipse console (see Figure 4.5).

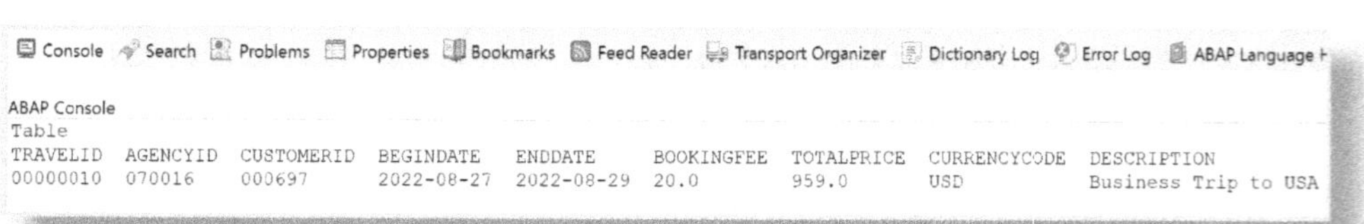

Figure 4.5: Read journey—edition

4.3 Updating data (UPDATE)

4.3.1 Syntax

The syntax for updating is similar to the syntax for reading data, using the ABAP language command `MODIFY ENTITIES OF`. We will now look at how to update data using a concrete example (see Listing 4.4). Note that in the subsequent operations—create and delete—modify operations always start with the language command `MODIFY ENTITIES OF`.

```
MODIFY ENTITIES OF z_c_travel
    ENTITY z_c_travel
    UPDATE FIELDS ( Description )
    WITH VALUE #( ( TravelId = '$ID'
                    Description = 'My great journey' ) )
    REPORTED DATA(lt_reported)
    FAILED DATA(lt_failed)
    MAPPED DATA(lt_mapped).
```

Listing 4.4: "MODIFY ENTITIES" syntax —updating data

The lines in this syntax are as follows:

- `MODIFY ENTITIES OF`—introduction line, including the behavior definition to be updated, `z_c_travel`.
- `ENTITY`—this keyword specifies the entity concerned, which in this example also has the name `z_c_travel`.
- The next line is crucial, as it defines the operation(s) to be executed. To update the data, we use the keyword `UPDATE` and then specify a list of `FIELDS (Description)` to be updated. These can be specified classically as an inline declaration in brackets, separated by spaces. Alternatively, a table with fields can also be specified.
- In the fourth line, in addition to the fields to be changed, the key fields of our entity `z_c_travel` must also be specified. In our example, we want to use our command to update the travel with the number `'$ID'` (key field `TravelId`). In doing so, we assign a new description `My great journey` in the `Description` field.
- Table types `REPORTED`, `FAILED` and `MAPPED` are also generated.

4.3.2 Implementation

For testing, we will overwrite the previous implementation in the ZCL_TRAVEL_SERVICE class. Using a concrete example, we will implement a method in a class that updates a description and displays the changed entry in the console in Eclipse. To do this, copy the ABAP code from Listing 4.5 into the method if_oo_adt_classrun~main.

```
METHOD if_oo_adt_classrun~main.

    MODIFY ENTITIES OF z_c_travel
        ENTITY z_c_travel
        UPDATE FIELDS ( Description )
        WITH VALUE #( ( TravelId = me->m_travel
                         Description = 'This is a test' ) )
        REPORTED DATA(lt_reported)
        FAILED DATA(lt_failed)
        MAPPED DATA(lt_mapped).
    IF lt_failed IS INITIAL.
      COMMIT ENTITIES.
      READ ENTITIES OF z_c_travel
        ENTITY z_c_travel
        ALL FIELDS WITH VALUE #( ( TravelId = me->m_travel )
)
        RESULT DATA(lt_travels).
      out->write(  data = lt_travels ).
    ELSE.
      ROLLBACK ENTITIES.
    ENDIF.

ENDMETHOD.
```

Listing 4.5: Update class for updating an entry

The implementation is simple. We first update the travel description field. If the internal table lt_failed remains empty, we confirm the execution with the language command COMMIT ENTITIES. We then read the same travel and output it in the Eclipse console. If errors occur during the update, the changes are reversed with the ROLLBACK ENTITIES statement. We can now test our implementation, as previously covered in Section 4.2.2.

If the change has been successful, the changed data set will appear with the new description text, as shown in Figure 4.6.

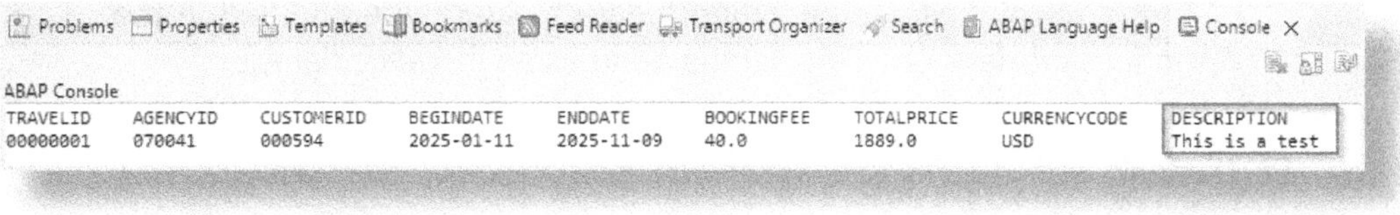

Figure 4.6: Updated data set

4.4 Creating data (CREATE)

4.4.1 Syntax

Having looked at the syntax for reading and updating data in the previous sections, we will now turn to the logic for creating data, using a specific example. We again use the ABAP command `MODIFY ENTITIES OF` (see Listing 4.6).

```
MODIFY ENTITIES OF z_c_travel
    ENTITY z_c_travel
    CREATE FIELDS ( Description )
    WITH VALUE #( ( TravelId = '$ID'
                    Description = 'Test' ) )
    FAILED DATA(lt_failed)
    REPORTED DATA(lt_reported)
    MAPPED DATA(lt_mapped).
```

Listing 4.6: "MODIFY ENTITIES" syntax —creating data

The lines are as follows:

- The introductory command `MODIFY ENTITIES OF` is followed by the behavior definition to be updated, `z_c_travel`.
- In the second line, we specify the affected entity with the name `z_c_travel`.
- The key difference can be seen in the third line—we now execute the create operation, using the keyword `CREATE`, followed by the `FIELDS (Description)`, that are to be created.

- In the fourth line, we specify the data to be created and fill in the entity's primary key. This can be done as an inline declaration:

```
WITH VALUE #((TravelId = '$ID' Description = 'Test')).
```

Alternatively, an internal table can be specified.

At this point, you might be wondering what the internal table type is, so that it can be used for the create operation. As part of the introduction of RAP, new ABAP keywords are available for the data type declaration. A suitable data type can be generated for our entities and the corresponding operation at runtime:

```
DATA: lt_create TYPE TABLE FOR CREATE z_c_travel.
```

In this coding, the name of the internal table (`lt_create`) is specified first, after the `DATA` statement, followed by the keywords `TYPE TABLE FOR`. Next, we specify the action `CREATE/UPDATE/ DELETE`, then the entity `Z_C_TRAVEL`.

New ABAP keywords

Various new ABAP keywords were introduced during RAP implementation. For further information, we recommend using the ABAP Language help function. Simply click on a keyword in the program code and press the function key [F1] to display the corresponding documentation.

The new data declaration instruction automatically generates a table data type that can be used for the EML interface. In Figure 4.7 you can see the generated type in the ABAP element info. The same components are offered for the inline declaration.

As we have not yet worked with deep structures in our previous examples and have only created one data record at a time via EML, the `%cid` field ❶ has not yet been required. This field is used to uniquely identify a data record in hierarchical data models.

Figure 4.7: "CREATE" operation—generated ABAP structure

In our example, we have directly defined the fields to be created with the command `CREATE FIELDS`—the structure `%control` ❷ has not previously been of interest. You can think of this structure as the X structure from a BAPI (Business Application Programming Interface). You need to mark the field name as changeable if its value is to be adopted when it is created. *Component groups* ❸ are also available within the structure for the simplified transfer of data values.

> **Generated data types—display**
>
> The generated data types in Figure 4.7 might look different depending on the operation. If you want to display the structure during development, click on the name of the variable and open the *ABAP Element Info* dialog box via function key [F2]. Alternatively, you can add the dialog to your standard display in Eclipse, via Eclipse menu path WINDOW • SHOW VIEW • OTHERS • ABAP ELEMENT INFO.

4.4.2 Implementation

In our example, we want to read out an existing travel, then copy it and assign a new `TravelId`. After it has been successfully created, we read the new travel and output it to the Eclipse console. To do this, we overwrite the implementation of the `main` method in the `zcl_travel_service` class (see Listing 4.7).

```
DATA: lt_create TYPE TABLE FOR CREATE z_c_travel.
READ ENTITIES OF z_c_travel
  ENTITY z_c_travel
  ALL FIELDS WITH VALUE #( ( travelid = me->m_travel ) )
  RESULT DATA(lt_result).
IF lt_result IS NOT INITIAL.
   lt_create = CORRESPONDING #( lt_result CHANGING CONTROL ).
   lt_create[ 1 ]-travelid = '99000001'.
   MODIFY ENTITIES OF z_c_travel
     ENTITY z_c_travel
     CREATE AUTO FILL CID
     WITH lt_create
     MAPPED DATA(lt_mapped)
     FAILED DATA(lt_failed)
     REPORTED DATA(lt_reported).
   IF lt_failed IS INITIAL.
     COMMIT ENTITIES.
     READ ENTITIES OF z_c_travel
         ENTITY z_c_travel
         ALL FIELDS WITH VALUE #( ( travelid = '99000001' ) )
         RESULT lt_result.
     out->write( lt_result ).
   ENDIF.
ENDIF.
```

Listing 4.7: Implementing the class for creating data

As shown in the implementation, we use the ABAP keyword `CORRESPONDING` to copy the data between two internal tables. In addition, we work with the `CHANGING CONTROL` statement, a new feature introduced with EML. As previously explained, the `%control fields` must be checked so that the values are transferred. To save a LOOP at this point, we can use the `CHANGING CONTROL` addition—the `%control` field is automatically set to `if_abap_behv=>mk-on` for the fields entered. Figure 4.8 shows an excerpt from the ABAP debugger. All fields marked with 01 are written. If the value is 00, the field value is not transferred.

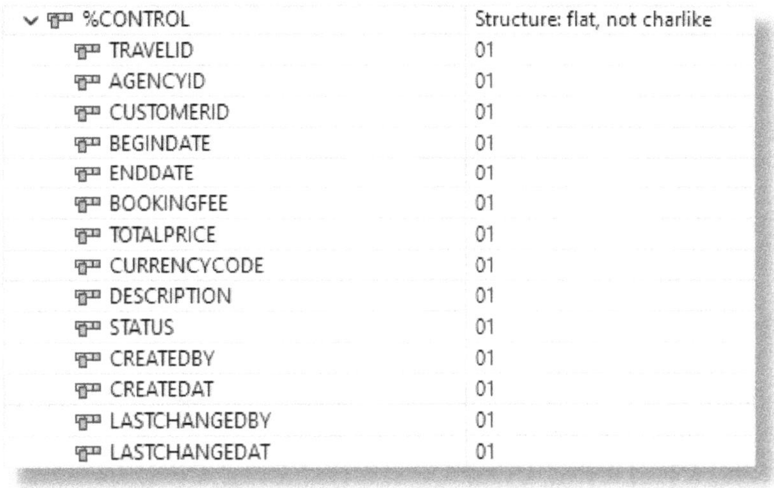

Figure 4.8: Setting field controls

After executing the class, we should see the newly created data set in the Eclipse console, as shown in Figure 4.9.

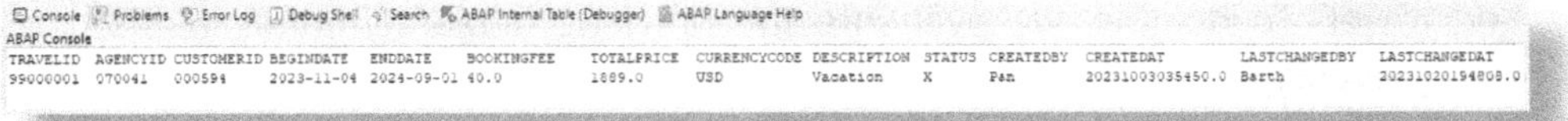

Figure 4.9: Newly created data set

4.5 Deleting data (DELETE)

4.5.1 Syntax

Now that we have familiarized ourselves with the change operations for creating and updating, we will now look at the last essential operation—deleting. Deleting is the easiest option to use in EML.

Once again, we start with the command `MODIFY ENTITIES OF` (see Listing 4.8).

```
MODIFY ENTITIES OF z_c_travel
  ENTITY z_c_travel
  DELETE FROM VALUE #( ( TravelId = '$ID' ) )
FAILED DATA(lt_failed)
REPORTED DATA(lt_reported)
MAPPED DATA(lt_mapped).
```

Listing 4.8: "MODIFY ENTITIES" syntax—deleting data

The only difference to the other two operations is the keyword `DELETE`, which specifies that the data record is to be deleted.

4.5.2 Implementation

In our implementation, we want to delete a data record from the entity `z_c_travel`. To confirm the deletion, we need to look up the deleted travel. To do this, we overwrite the previous implementation in the `ZCL_TRAVEL_SERVICE` class (see Listing 4.9).

```
  METHOD if_oo_adt_classrun~main.
    MODIFY ENTITIES OF z_c_travel
      ENTITY z_c_travel
      DELETE FROM VALUE #( ( travelid = me->m_travel ) )
    FAILED DATA(lt_failed)
    REPORTED DATA(lt_reported)
    MAPPED DATA(lt_mapped).
    IF lt_failed IS INITIAL.
```

```
      COMMIT ENTITIES.

      READ ENTITIES OF z_c_travel
        ENTITY z_c_travel
        ALL FIELDS WITH VALUE #( ( travelid = me->m_travel )
)
      RESULT DATA(lt_result).
      IF lt_result IS INITIAL.
        out->write( 'Entry successfully deleted' ).
      ENDIF.
    ENDIF.
  ENDMETHOD.
```

Listing 4.9: Implementing a class to delete an entry

In the next step, we can execute the class as a console application. If the execution is successful, we will receive a message in the console, as shown in Figure 4.10.

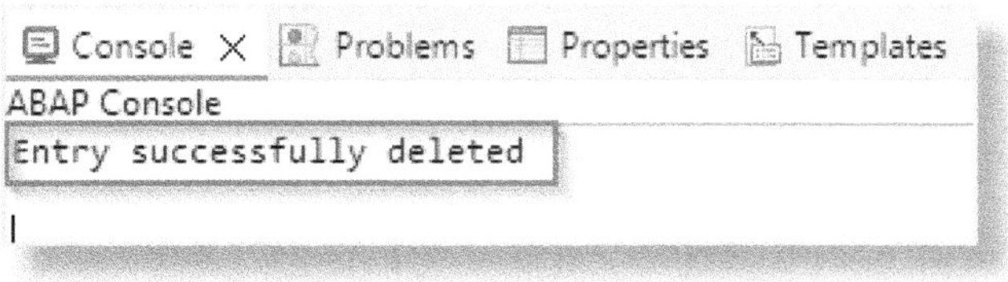

Figure 4.10: Deletion of the entry—success message

4.6 Summary

In this chapter, we covered the RAP model "travel" as a basis for the introduction to EML—from the definition of the data structure to the provision of a RESTful service. We introduced the new ABAP language commands that are used in the RAP model, and we focused on accessing the transactional buffer using EML and the ability to perform CRUD operations directly from ABAP programs. This enables efficient reuse of code for BOs, both in applications and in programmatic contexts.

5 Methodologies in the ABAP RESTful Application Programming Model

This chapter covers advanced methodologies, such as numbering, determinations, validations, dynamic feature controls, actions, functions, the unmanaged save method, and hierarchies. These enable developers to design applications with increased flexibility, scalability and performance.

We will now explore the possibilities offered by RAP and learn how these methodologies help to efficiently develop and optimize applications. So, let's continue our journey.

5.1 Numbering

5.1.1 General principles

In databases, numbering refers to the automatic assignment of unique primary keys in RAP-BO. For specific processes, a user might want to enter the key manually. For others, numbering plays a secondary role and may also contain gaps. In certain contexts, there is a legal requirement for consecutive numbering that must not contain any gaps. RAP has solutions for all these different cases, which we will now examine.

There are three different types of numbering, which we will explore and compare in this section. Numbering is performed for a CDS view's primary key. This consists of one or more fields that are described with the key statement (see Listing 5.1).

```
define root view entity Z_I_TRAVEL
as select from /dmo/travel
{
key travel_id as TravelId
...
}
```

Listing 5.1: Defining primary key for "travel_id"

In the example, the `travel_id` field was defined as the primary key for the root view entity `Z_I_TRAVEL`

Early, late and external numbering

Early numbering sets the primary key values directly after the `CREATE` request is called. The values can be assigned by the RAP framework, programmatically via the *for-numbering* method or by user input from the frontend (external numbering). We will discuss implementation of the *for-numbering* method later in this chapter.

Early numbering is implemented with the `early numbering` command in the behavior definition (see Listing 5.2).

```
define behavior for Z_I_TRAVEL //alias <alias_name>
persistent table /DMO/TRAVEL
lock master
authorization master ( instance )
early numbering
{
[ . . . ]
}
```

Listing 5.2: Implementing early numbering

Late numbering is called during the storage process at the last point during storage—the "point of no return". At this point, the consistency of the BO has already been confirmed and the storage sequence triggered. This ensures that there are no gaps in the numbering and that the next number is always determined. Late numbering is implemented in the behavior definition with the `late numbering` command (see Listing 5.3).

```
define behavior for Z_I_TRAVEL //alias <alias_name>
persistent table /DMO/TRAVEL
lock master
authorization master ( instance )
late numbering
{
...
}
```

Listing 5.3: Implementing late numbering

Managed and unmanaged numbering

There are two types of numbering—managed numbering and unmanaged numbering.

With *managed numbering*, a number is assigned by the RAP framework. This is a UUID (Universally Unique Identifier) in RAW16 format. This automatic numbering is assigned in the behavior definition with the command `numbering : managed` for a UUID field, as follows:

```
field (numbering : managed) UUID;
```

Managed numbering was originally only possible in an early numbering implementation. SAP S/4HANA version 2022 FPS00 allowed it for the first time in a late numbering scenario.

Unmanaged numbering is used for individual number assignment and must be implemented in the behavior definition using ABAP code.

5.1.2 Implementation

We will now implement late numbering, which will assign the next free number as the `TravelId`.

To do this, we first open the behavior definition for the root view entity `Z_I_TRAVEL`. We then insert the `late numbering` command, as shown in Figure 5.1.

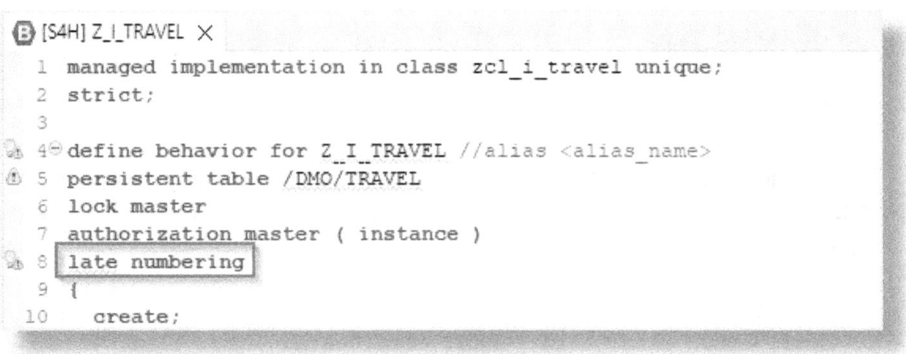

Figure 5.1: Inserting "late numbering" command

The quick fix symbol ( ) is then displayed. We can view the suggestion by using keyboard combination Ctrl + 1 or by clicking on the symbol (see Figure 5.2).

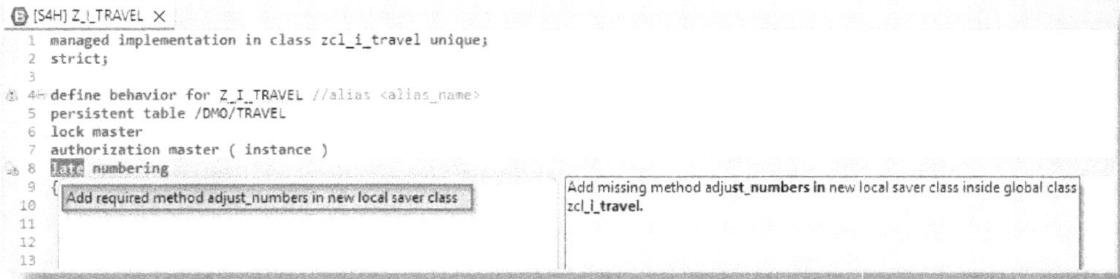

Figure 5.2: View of quick fix

We can confirm the quick fix by double-clicking with our mouse or pressing the Enter key. This automatically creates the ADJUST_NUMBERS method in the local class implementation of the ZCL_I_TRAVEL class (see Figure 5.3).

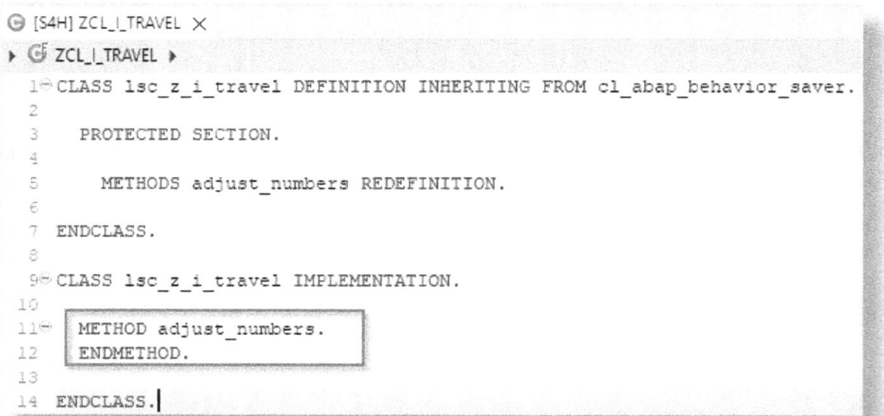

Figure 5.3: "Adjust_numbers" method

In this method, we want to assign the next free number by selecting the maximum `TravelId` from the database table `/DMO/TRAVEL` and incrementing it by one (see Listing 5.4).

```
METHOD adjust_numbers.
  SELECT MAX( travel_id ) FROM /dmo/travel
  INTO @DATA(lv_max).
    LOOP AT mapped-z_i_travel ASSIGNING
    FIELD-SYMBOL(<ls_travel>).
```

```
      lv_max = lv_max + 1.
      <ls_travel>-TravelId = lv_max.
    ENDLOOP.
ENDMETHOD.
```

Listing 5.4: "Adjust_numbers" method—coding

We then create a new travel in the frontend, leaving the TRAVEL ID field blank (see Figure 5.4).

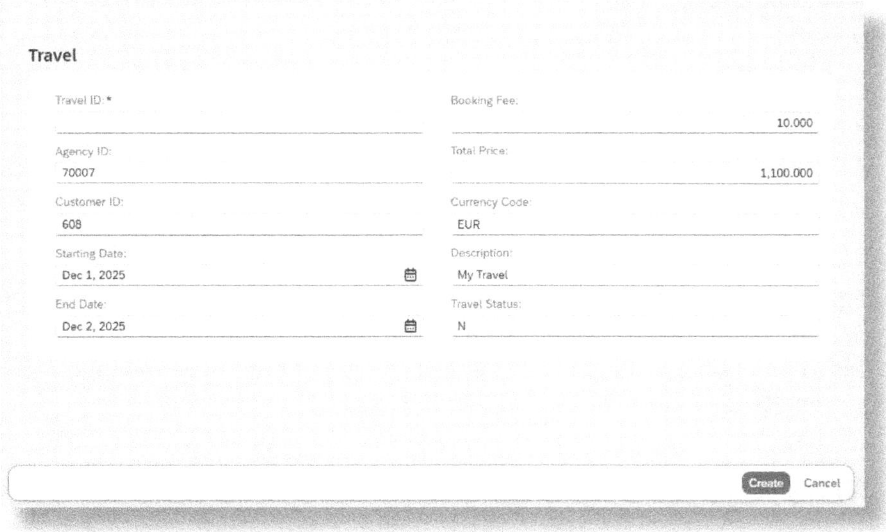

Figure 5.4: Creating new travel

After it has been created, the next free TRAVEL ID is automatically set correctly for the entry (see Figure 5.5).

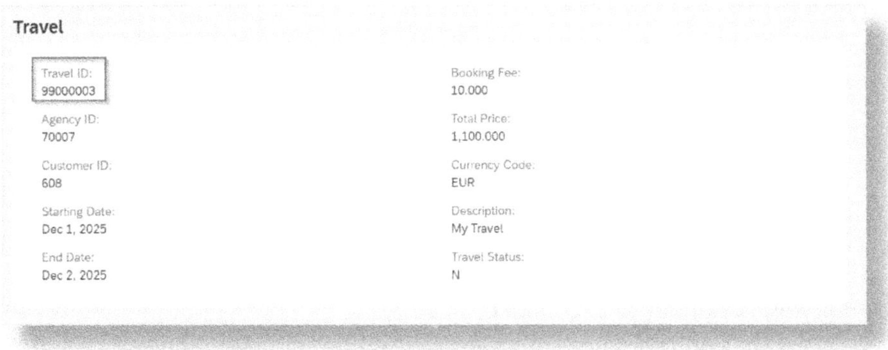

Figure 5.5: Successful assignment of the Travel ID

In the last step, it makes sense to set the TRAVEL ID field as `readonly` (read only) so that a user cannot assign their own ID for the travel. To do this, we include a corresponding addition to the instruction block in the behavior definition—`field (readonly) TravelId` (see Listing 5.5).

```
managed implementation in class zcl_i_travel unique;
strict;
define behavior for Z_I_TRAVEL //alias <alias_name>
persistent table /DMO/TRAVEL
lock master
authorization master ( instance )
late numbering
{
  create;
  update;
  delete;
  field (readonly) TravelId;
 [ . . . ]
}
```

Listing 5.5: Behavior definition "Z_I_TRAVEL"

This instruction causes the field to be displayed as not ready for input in the frontend (see Figure 5.6).

Figure 5.6: "Travel ID" field is displayed as "readonly"

5.2 Determinations

5.2.1 General principles

In the world of RAP, *determinations* play a crucial role when it comes to modifying instances of BO based on trigger conditions. Simply put, these are rules that automatically perform certain data calculations or changes to BO instances when specified conditions are met, such as when certain fields have been modified. Determinations are an optional part of the behavior of a BO and are called implicitly by its framework.

The trigger condition is evaluated at the time of the call—a predefined time during the runtime of the BO. A called determination can calculate data, modify entity instances according to the calculation result, and return messages to the consumer by passing them to the corresponding table in the REPORTED structure.

> **Special runtime aspects**
>
> - In unmanaged scenarios, determinations are only supported for draft instances, not for active instances.
> - The result of the determination must not change if the determination is carried out several times under the same conditions.
> - The execution sequence of determinations is not fixed. If more than one determination is triggered by the same condition, it is not known which determination will be executed first.
> - Once a determination has been triggered, it must be executed independently of other determinations.

5.2.2 Determinations with respect to RAP

We are now going to implement a new determination called `setDefaultBeginDate`, which is used to set the system date as the default value for the start date (BEGINDATE) of the new travel instance when it is created. The determination is automatically activated when the user creates a new travel instance.

First, we define the determination in the behavior definition *Z_I_TRAVEL*. To do this, insert the following statement into the main entity's define-behavior clause:

```
determination setDefaultBeginDate on modify { create; }
```

This specifies that determination of the `setDefaultBeginDate` is triggered by a modifying operation and restricts it with a subsequent operation specification. In our example, the trigger condition is a `create` operation.

After subsequent activation of the behavior definition, an Eclipse quick fix icon ( ) ❶ appears in the same line as the `determination` (see Figure 5.7). It can be triggered with a left-click, which creates the method in the behavior implementation.

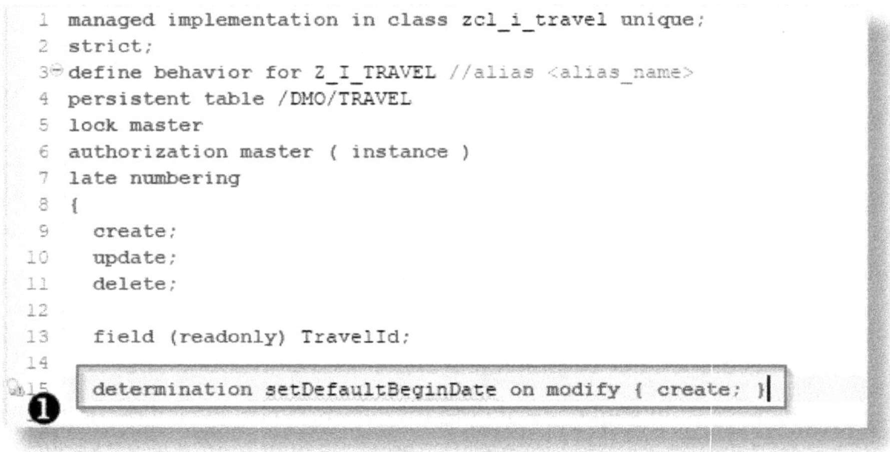

Figure 5.7: Definition—determination

A pop-up window then appears that offers the option to initiate automatic method creation, as shown at ❶ in Figure 5.8.

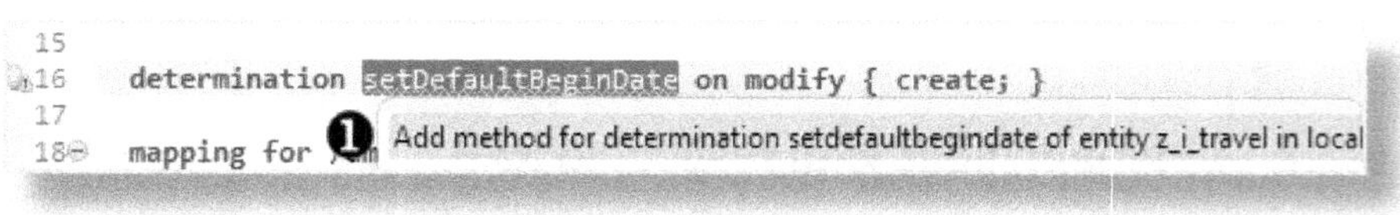

Figure 5.8: Quick fix—determination

We should now see the class with the behavior implementation, where the system automatically navigates us to the newly generated determination method. We then implement the `setdefaultbegindate` method with the functionality shown in Listing 5.6.

```
METHOD setdefaultbegindate.
    READ ENTITIES OF z_i_travel
      IN LOCAL MODE
      ENTITY z_i_travel
      ALL FIELDS WITH CORRESPONDING #( keys )
      RESULT DATA(lt_read_results)
      FAILED DATA(lt_failed)
      .
```

```
    MODIFY ENTITIES OF z_i_travel
      IN LOCAL MODE
      ENTITY z_i_travel
      UPDATE FIELDS ( BeginDate ) WITH VALUE #( FOR result
IN lt_read_results (
        %tky = result-%tky
        begindate = COND #(
          WHEN result-begindate IS INITIAL THEN sy-datum
          ELSE result-begindate
        )
      )
      )
      REPORTED DATA(lt_reported_from_update)
      FAILED DATA(lt_failed_from_update)
      MAPPED DATA(lt_mapped_from_update).

    reported = CORRESPONDING #( DEEP lt_reported_from_update
).
ENDMETHOD.
```

Listing 5.6: Method "setdefaultbegindate"—Determination

We read the start date (`BeginDate`) of the instances. If it is `INITIAL`, the `sy-datum` is written to this field. In this process, we use the EML statements `READ` and `MODIFY`, which were discussed in Chapter 4.

We can now switch to the Fiori preview and test our code. We create a new object and deliberately leave the STARTING DATE attribute blank, as shown in Figure 5.9.

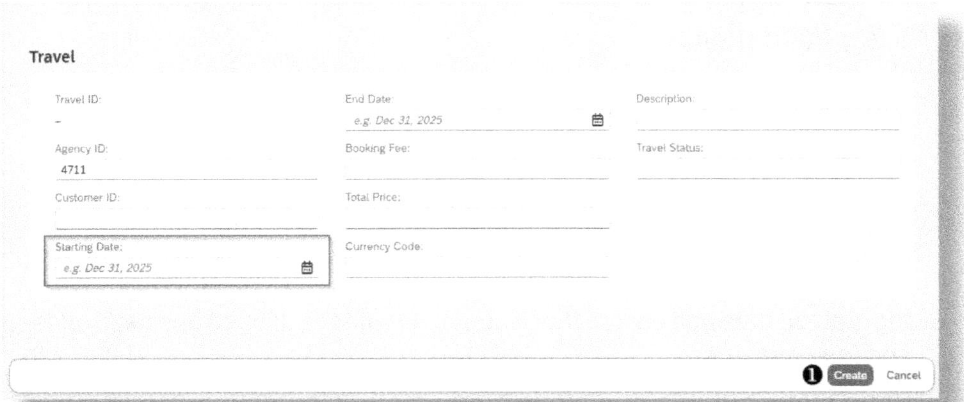

Figure 5.9: Testing—determination

The previously created object is then shown (see Figure 5.10). March 26, 2025 was entered as the `BeginDate` or STARTING DATE. In this scenario, this was the system date (variable `sy-datum`).

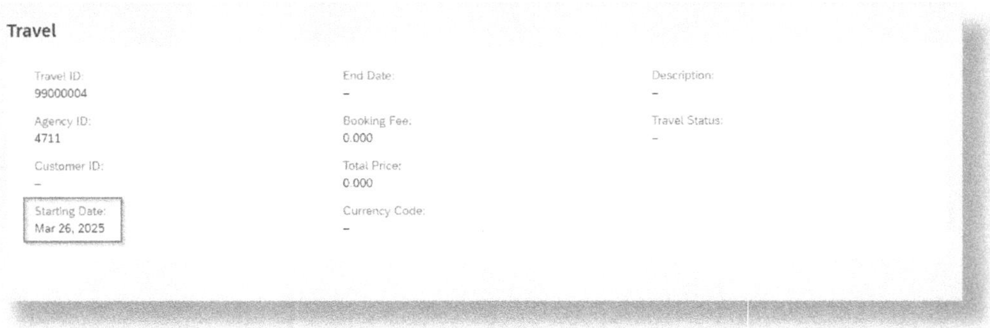

Figure 5.10: Result—determination

The use of determinations in the RAP enables flexible control of modifications to instances of BOs, based on defined trigger conditions. In this example, the determination method `setDefaultBeginDate` was implemented to set the system date for the STARTING DATE field (`BeginDate`) when creating a new travel instance. The trigger condition is fulfilled when a new instance is created.

Determinations' runtime aspects and the possibility of activation only for draft instances are all taken into account. Definition and implementation of the determination takes place in the main entity object's behavior definition. This highlights the flexibility and power of determinations in the RAP framework.

5.3 Validations

5.3.1 General principles

Validations are a crucial part of the data processing process in a BO. They are executed during the storage sequence of a BO and serve to ensure the integrity and correctness of the data. The purpose of a validation is to check the entered data and ensure that it complies with the defined business rules and requirements.

If validation detects an error, an interruption of the save sequence is triggered. The system signals to the user that a correction is required before the save process can be continued. This interruption is essential because it prevents invalid or incorrect data from being transferred to the system, which ultimately leads to more reliable and efficient business processes.

A distinction is made between general validations and validations at field level. With a *general validation*, the validation is run every time a BO is changed. This means that regardless of which specific fields have been changed, the entire validation logic is executed. This is particularly useful if several fields in an object are interdependent or if the validation affects the overall structure of the object.

In contrast, a *validation at field level* is only carried out if the value of a specific field has changed. This type of validation is more efficient if only individual fields need to be checked and there are no dependencies on other parts of the object. It enables focused validation, which saves resources and speeds up the processing procedure.

Validation syntax

A validation is defined in the behavior definition with the `validation` command, followed by the name (<NAME>) of the validation and the triggering event (`<OPTIONS>`), as shown below:

```
validation <NAME> on save { <OPTIONS> }
```

As mentioned previously, validation can be restricted to individual fields. A `field` statement is used for this purpose. In addition, `create`, `update` or `delete` statements can be used to specify that the validation is only triggered by the corresponding change operations. If no such specification is made, validation is carried out for every change operation.

5.3.2 Implementation

In our example, we would like to implement a validation for the currency field to ensure that only EUR (euro) is accepted as currency.

To do this, we create a validation at field level for the `CurrencyCode` field:

```
validation checkCurrency on save { field CurrencyCode; }
```

In Eclipse, the quick fix icon ( ) is again displayed (see Figure 5.11). We can view the system's proposal either by clicking on the icon or by using key combination Ctrl + 1.

Figure 5.11: Validation—proposal

Confirm the quick fix by double-clicking or pressing the Enter key.

We then use the EML `READ ENTITIES OF` statement to read the entries that are to be validated, and check which currency was entered in each case (see Listing 5.7).

```
METHOD checkCurrency.
  READ ENTITIES OF z_i_travel
    IN LOCAL MODE
    ENTITY z_i_travel
    ALL FIELDS WITH CORRESPONDING #( keys )
    RESULT DATA(lt_read_results)
    FAILED DATA(lt_failed_results).

  LOOP AT lt_read_results ASSIGNING
  FIELD-SYMBOL(<ls_result>).
    IF <ls_result>-CurrencyCode <> 'EUR'.
      INSERT VALUE #(
         %pid = <ls_result>-%pid
         travelid = <ls_result>-TravelId
      ) INTO TABLE failed-z_i_travel.

      INSERT VALUE #(
         %pid = <ls_result>-%pid
         travelid = <ls_result>-TravelId
         %msg = new_message_with_text(
          severity = if_abap_behv_message=>severity-error
          text = 'Only Euro is accepted as currency'
         )
         %element-currencycode = if_abap_behv=>mk-on
      ) INTO TABLE reported-z_i_travel.
```

```
    ENDIF.
  ENDLOOP.
ENDMETHOD.
```

Listing 5.7: "checkCurrency" method

For entries where `EUR` is not set as the currency, we add the key values to the generated `failed` structure. In addition, we create a new entry with a message in the `%msg` component of the generated reported structure. To mark the affected field in the application, we set the value of the constant `if_abap_behv=>mk-on` in the `%element` component's `currencycode` field.

As a result, an error message appears in the application if we enter and save a currency other than *EUR* in the frontend (see Figure 5.12).

Figure 5.12: Error message received—frontend validation successful

With the implementation complete, we have created an effective method to ensure that only a *EUR* value is accepted in the currency field. This validation is a crucial part of maintaining data integrity and ensuring consistent business processes. Our example illustrates how precise and focused data validation is implemented within the RAP model—a fundamental element in developing robust and reliable SAP applications. With such customized validations, developers can increase the quality of user interactions while ensuring the stability and reliability of the systems. This approach, combined with the flexibility and efficiency of the RAP model, provides us with a strong foundation for future development and optimizations.

5.4 Actions

5.4.1 General principles

An action is a *post* operation (changing access) in the behavior definition. It can have a reference to an entity from the BO, but does not have to. The advantage of an action is that you do not have to switch to the change mode of an individual entity and can therefore make changes to a BO without specifically editing the entity. It is possible to incorporate logic of any complexity into an action that is not related to the actual BO.

An action is defined with an `action` statement, and a name (`<NAME>`) is assigned for the action. You can also optionally assign a parameter (`<ENTITY>`), a return cardinality (`<C>`), and a return entity (`<ENTITY>`):

```
action <NAME> parameter <ENTITY> result [<C>] <ENTITY>;
```

Different types of actions

There are different types of actions, and we would like to briefly explain the differences between them.

Actions

An *action* has a reference to the entity, and the key fields of the entity are automatically passed through to the action so that a connection to the selected lines in the frontend can be established. The command in the behavior definition for this is `action`. An example would be updating the travel status for the selected travels in the frontend, as follows:

```
action setTravelAccepted result [1] $self;
```

Internal actions

Actions can normally also be called externally; for example, via an ODATA request. However, it is possible for actions to be called only within the business logic of the same BO. *Internal actions* are used for this, and the command is `internal action` in the behavior definition. An example would be the recalculation of prices when the currency changes:

```
internal action calcPriceForCurrency result [1] $self;
```

Static actions

A *static* action is detached from the implementing entity and does not require any reference to it. The behavior definition contains the `static action` command for this. An example would be the cancellation of all existing travels, whereby no explicit reference to a line is required:

```
static action cancelAllTravel;
```

Factory actions

The *instance-based factory action* is suitable for copying processes, because existing values are copied from an existing instance. Default values can be adopted with a *static factory action*. The command for this is `factory action` in the behavior definition.

An example of an instance-based factory action would be a copy of an existing travel. The return cardinality of a factory action is always `[1]`:

```
factory action copyTravel [1];
```

! Release dependency

The feature for instance-based factory actions is only available as of SAP S/4HANA version 2022 FPS00.

5.4.2 Implementation

In the next example, we will implement a static action that sets all travels for a customer to "canceled".

We will specifically create a pop-up for entering a customer number in the frontend and then set all travels for the customer number entered to status *X* (canceled).

First, we need to define an abstract entity for entering the customer number. To do this, we create a DATA DEFINITION in Eclipse (see Figure 5.13). We assign a NAME (*Z_A_CANCEL_TRAVEL*) ❶ and a DESCRIPTION ❷, and confirm by clicking on NEXT ❸.

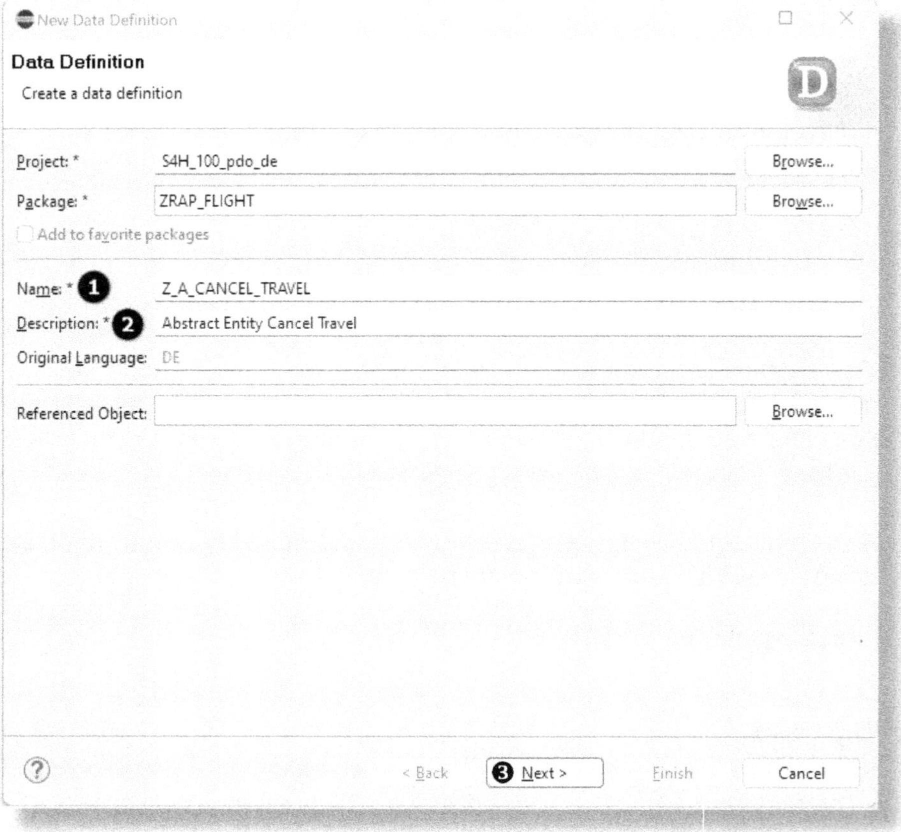

Figure 5.13: Creating a data definition

> **Abstract entity**
>
> An *abstract entity* is a structure without a reference to a database table. This is often used when parameters are going to be transferred from or to an action or function.

After selecting the transport, we select the TEMPLATE—*Define Abstract Entity with Parameters* ❶—and confirm by clicking on FINISH ❷, as shown in Figure 5.14.

Figure 5.14: Selecting a template for the abstract entity

We then add the `CustomerId` component to enter the customer number to the abstract entity and we delete the automatically generated statement for parameters from the abstract entity (see Listing 5.8).

```
@EndUserText.label: 'Abstract Entity Cancel Travel'
define abstract entity Z_A_CANCEL_TRAVEL
{
   key CustomerId : /dmo/customer_id;
}
```

Listing 5.8: "CustomerId" component

In the next step, we create a new static action in the behavior definition *Z_I_TRAVEL* with the abstract entity as a parameter:

```
static action cancelTravel parameter Z_A_CANCEL_TRAVEL;
```

After defining the action, we can start it with the quick fix icon ( ), as shown in Figure 5.15, and it can be implemented in the class.

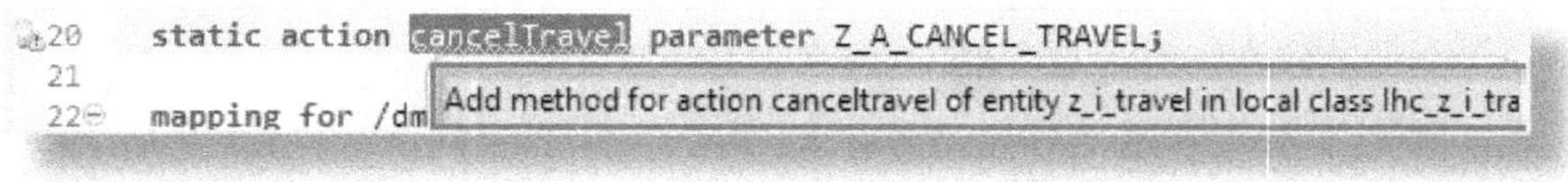

Figure 5.15: Quick fix to implement the action

Before implementing the action, it must be added to the projection view `Z_C_TRAVEL` using command `use action` (see Listing 5.9).

```
projection;
strict;

define behavior for Z_C_TRAVEL //alias <alias_name>
{
  use create;
  use update;
  use delete;

  use action cancelTravel;
}
```

Listing 5.9: Behavior definition "Z_C_TRAVEL" —use action

The function now has to be integrated as an action in the CDS view `Z_C_TRAVEL`. To do this, we add the `lineItem` annotation for the `Status` field (see Listing 5.10).

```
@UI: { lineItem: [{ position: 100 },{ type: #FOR_ACTION,
dataAction: 'cancelTravel', label: 'Cancel Travel' }],
identification: [{ position: 100 }] }
  Status,
```

Listing 5.10: "Status" field —"lineItem" annotation

In the last step, we implement the action in the program code by including the coding in `METHOD cancelTravel` (see Listing 5.11).

```
METHOD cancelTravel.
LOOP AT keys INTO DATA(ls_keys).
  SELECT * FROM /dmo/travel WHERE customer_id = @ls_keys-%param-
CustomerId INTO TABLE @DATA(lt_travels).
  IF sy-subrc = 0.
    LOOP AT lt_travels INTO DATA(ls_travel).
      UPDATE /dmo/travel SET Status = 'X' WHERE travel_id = @ls_
travel-travel_id.
      IF sy-subrc = 0.
        APPEND VALUE #( travelid = ls_travel-travel_id %cid = ls_
keys-%cid ) TO mapped-z_i_travel.
        APPEND VALUE #( travelid = ls_travel-travel_id %cid = ls_
keys-%cid
                        %msg = new_message_with_text( severity =
if_abap_behv_message=>severity-success
                                                      text =
'Travel' && | | && ls_travel-travel_id && | | && 'successfully
updated' ) ) TO reported-z_i_travel.
      ELSE.
        APPEND VALUE #( travelid = ls_travel-travel_id %cid = ls_
keys-%cid ) TO failed-z_i_travel.
        APPEND VALUE #( travelid = ls_travel-travel_id %cid = ls_
keys-%cid
                        %msg = new_message_with_text( severity =
if_abap_behv_message=>severity-error
                                                      text = 'Error
for Travel ' && | | && ls_travel-travel_id ) ) TO reported-z_i_
travel.
      ENDIF.
    ENDLOOP.
  ENDIF.
ENDLOOP.
ENDMETHOD.
```

Listing 5.11: Method "cancelTravel"

If we now switch to the frontend, we can see the defined static action CANCEL TRAVEL above the table display, as shown in Figure 5.16.

Figure 5.16 Action—"Cancel Travel"

Clicking on the action opens a pop-up, where we enter the CUSTOMER ID (see Figure 5.17).

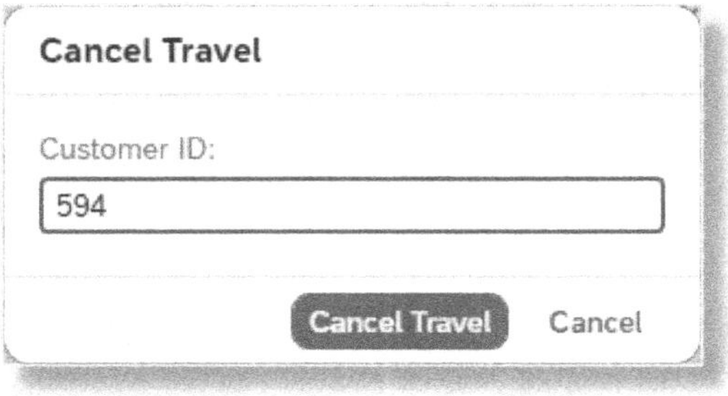

Figure 5.17: "Cancel Travel"—entering customer ID

After the action has been executed using the CANCEL TRAVEL action button, the system reports which travels have been successfully updated (see Figure 5.18).

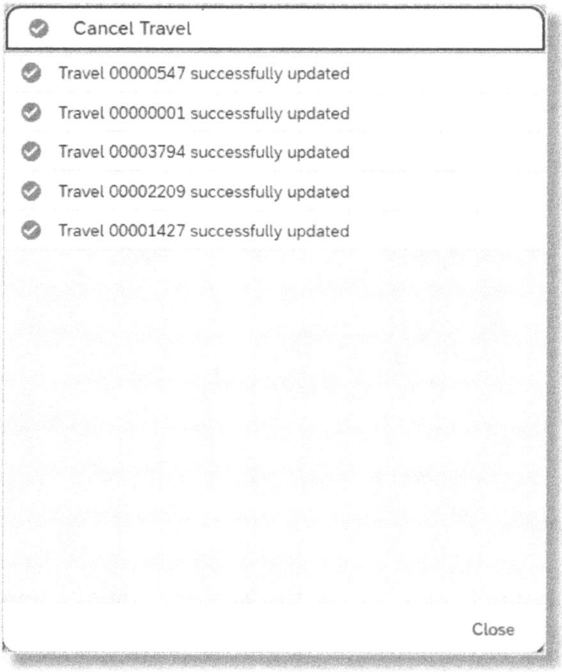

Figure 5.18: Overview of updates made

As we have seen, actions offer us an easy way to trigger complex business logic without having to make any changes to the actual BO.

5.5 Functions

5.5.1 General principles

A *function* is a get operation (read access) that is specified in the behavior definition. It can have a reference to an entity from the BO, but it does not have to. A function is defined in the same way as an action, using the `function` command and a name for the function (`<NAME>`). Optional parameters can be assigned—(`<ENTITY>`), a return cardinality (`<C>`), and a return entity (`<ENTITY>`).

```
function <NAME> parameter <ENTITY> result [<C>] <ENTITY>;
```

Different types of functions

The differences between actions and functions are mainly in the HTTP method. *POST* is used for actions, whereas *GET* is used for functions. At this point, we will now look at examples of different uses of functions, which can be divided into two types—functions and static functions.

Functions

A *function* executes a context-dependent operation based on the lines selected in the frontend. It is designated in the behavior definition with the `function` command. An example would be the output of the number of travels per customer number:

```
function countTravel result [1..*] $self;
```

Static functions

A *static function* is detached from the actual entity and does not require any reference to its key fields. The command in the behavior definition for this is `static function`. It could be used, for example, to read default values from the backend when creating a new travel:

```
static function defaultValues result [1] $self;
```

5.5.2 Implementation

As an example, we will now implement a context-dependent function that determines the customer number for the travel selected in the frontend. The number of travels for the customer number is then output as information in a *message toast* notification.

In the behavior definition, we create the new function `countTravel` with the return parameter `[1..*] $self;`

```
function countTravel result [1..*] $self;
```

The function is then activated via the quick fix icon ( ), as shown in Figure 5.19, and is then implemented in the class.

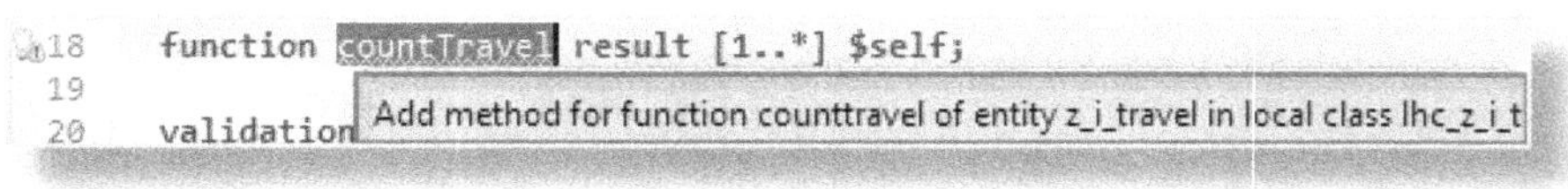

Figure 5.19: Applying the method using quick fix

We can then add the coding for the function that outputs the number of travels per customer number (see Listing 5.12).

```
  METHOD counttravel.
    READ ENTITIES OF z_i_travel
      IN LOCAL MODE
      ENTITY z_i_travel
      ALL FIELDS WITH CORRESPONDING #( keys )
      RESULT DATA(lt_read_results)
      FAILED DATA(lt_failed_results).

    LOOP AT lt_read_results INTO DATA(ls_result).
      SELECT COUNT(*) FROM z_i_travel WHERE customerid = @
ls_result-customerid INTO @DATA(lv_travels).
      IF sy-subrc = 0.
        APPEND VALUE #( travelid = ls_result-travelid %pid =
ls_result-%pid ) TO result.
        APPEND VALUE #( travelid = ls_result-travelid %pid =
ls_result-%pid
                        %msg = new_message_with_text( severity =
if_abap_behv_message=>severity-information
```

```
                                                       text =
|The Customer | && ls_result-CustomerId && | has | && lv_
travels && | Travels| ) ) TO reported-z_i_travel.
      ENDIF.
    ENDLOOP.
  ENDMETHOD.
```

Listing 5.12: METHOD "counttravel"

In the next step, we make the function available in the projection behavior definition Z_C_TRAVEL. To do this, we use the `use function` command (see Listing 5.13).

```
projection;
strict;

define behavior for Z_C_TRAVEL //alias <alias_name>
{
  use create;
  use update;
  use delete;

  use action cancelTravel;
  use function countTravel;
}
```

Listing 5.13: Behavior definition "Z_C_TRAVEL"—function

As a final step, we need to insert an annotation for the function in the projection CDS view `Z_C_TRAVEL`. We use the same annotation as for actions. To do this, the annotation is added above the `CustomerId` field at `lineItem` level (see Listing 5.14).

```
@UI: { lineItem: [{ position: 30 },{ type: #FOR_ACTION,
dataAction: 'countTravel', label: 'Count Travel' }],
identification: [{ position: 30 }], selectionField: [{
position: 20 }] }
  CustomerId,
```

Listing 5.14: View Z_C_TRAVEL—annotation for the function

The new COUNT TRAVEL function is now displayed in the frontend (see Figure 5.20). It is initially inactive and appears grayed out—a line (context) needs to be selected for execution.

Figure 5.20: New "Count Travel" function in the frontend

Once this has been done, we can click on the COUNT TRAVEL button, which is now active (see Figure 5.21).

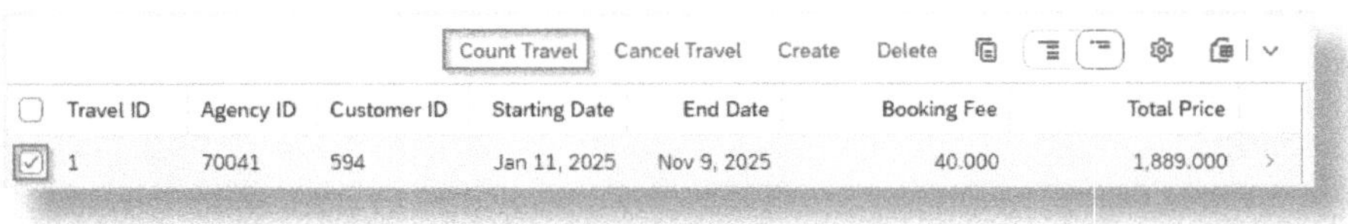

Figure 5.21: Executing "Count Travel" function

After execution, a message toast notification appears, showing the number of travels for the corresponding customer number, as shown in Figure 5.22.

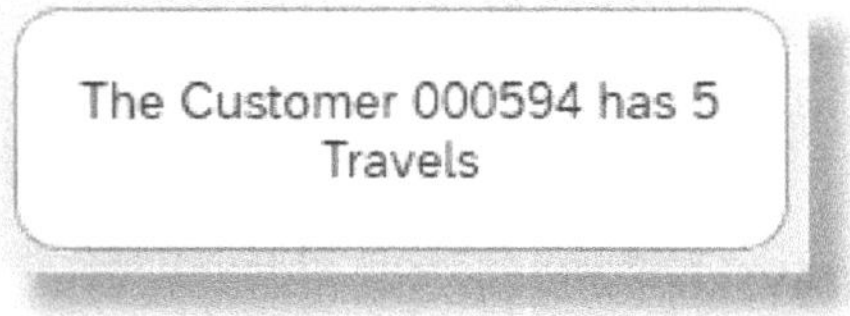

Figure 5.22: Notification—number of travels

5.6 Feature control

5.6.1 General principles

Feature control defines how data and operations are made accessible in the service. This control enables entity operations and attributes to be conditionally deactivated or hidden. Fiori Elements reads this information from the service's metadata so that specific operations and fields are shown or hidden as required. These flexible settings enable developers to protect sensitive data and only make it visible to appropriate users.

Feature control can be implemented in two ways:

- *Statically*—with the *static* variant (static feature control), you definitively determine which operations will be available for each BO entity and which fields will have specific access restrictions (e.g., the mandatory fields or read-only fields).
- *Dynamically*—*dynamic* feature control, on the other hand, means that access restrictions for fields, or the activation/deactivation of methods, depend on the status of the BO (e.g., on the value of a certain field).

In UI scenarios, the data retrieved from the backend provides the UI with information about which operations are currently activated. In Fiori Elements UI, operation buttons are only clickable if authorization and feature control methods deliver a positive result under the current conditions (the state of the retrieved BO instances).

It is important to define and implement authorization and feature control methods because the calculations performed are based on their results. When displaying the list report or object page for a specific instance, the authorization and feature control implementation methods are called. Authorization for all actions is checked in advance. As a result, users cannot start operations for which they are not authorized because their triggers (action buttons) are not available.

This function is provided by the RAP framework, but its use is not mandatory. It can be added as an option to the existing functions. Feature control can be applied to fields to influence certain properties, but can also be applied to standard operations (e.g. update, delete) and to actions/functions that need to be activated or deactivated.

There are two ways to implement feature control:

- *Instance-based feature* (`features:instance`)—the data of the individual instances is available. A decision is made per instance as to how the feature is handled.
- *Global feature* (`features:global`)—there is no access to the specific data of individual instances. Instead, a one-off, global decision is made as to whether a feature can be used or not. This decision then applies uniformly to all instances.

Note that a behavior definition can contain several entities. The selected feature control (instance-based or global) then applies to all entities included in the behavior definition. The choice depends on the application requirements.

Dynamic feature control in an instance-based context makes it possible to dynamically control the display and availability of data fields, operations, or actions depending on the status of a BO instance. Unlike static feature control, where the restrictions cannot be changed, access to certain functions or fields in dynamic feature control depends on the runtime conditions of an instance.

Some key aspects of dynamic feature control in an instance-based context include:

- *State-dependent control*—access to certain functions or fields can be influenced by trigger conditions that react to changes in the state of the instance. These triggers can be based on modification processes or changed fields.
- *Runtime control*—in contrast to static feature control, which is defined during development, dynamic features are controlled during runtime. This enables flexible adaptation in response to changes in the BO's behavior.
- *Individual instance handling*—each instance of a BO can be handled individually. The dynamic feature control enables different restrictions or display properties to be defined for each instance.
- *Application-related customizations*—dynamic feature control provides granular control that is well suited for application-based customizations. For example, an operation can be activated/deactivated depending on certain conditions.

5.6.2 Implementation

As an example, we are going to deactivate the functions for updating and deleting travels with the status "N" (New).

We will now turn our attention to the development of dynamic feature control. To do this, we extend the `delete` and `update` methods. These operations are always active when a data set is selected. However, our aim is to change these operations so that execution is only guaranteed if the status of the entity is not equal to "N". To achieve this, we include the corresponding feature in the operations in the behavior definition:

```
update (features : instance);
delete (features : instance);
```

Once the instance features have been defined, the Eclipse quick fix icon ( ) appears, as shown at ❶ in Figure 5.23. We initiate it by left clicking and selecting the action ADD. METHOD FOR OPERATION INSTANCE_FEATURES ON ENTITY Z_I_TRAVEL IN LOCAL CLASS ❷ to create the method for the instance features.

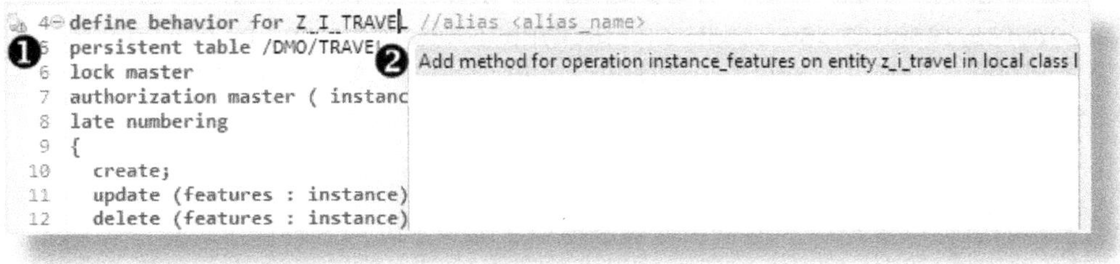

Figure 5.23: Creating feature control

The method we just generated carries "new" parameters, as shown in Figure 5.24.

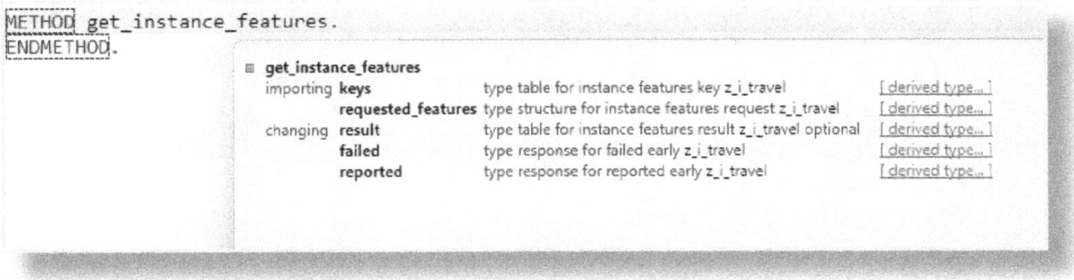

Figure 5.24: "get_instance_features" method

Some of the key details in the image are:

- `for instance features`—this clause in the method signature indicates that this is an instance method used for dynamic feature control at instance level. This means that the feature control is performed based on the data of a specific instance.
- `importing keys`—this parameter is a table with the instance keys to which the feature control is applied.
- `importing requested_features`—information is provided about which elements of the entity (fields and operations) have been requested by the caller for the feature control.

- `changing result`—is used to save the result of the feature control performed.
- `changing failed`—this parameter contains information to identify the data record for which an error has occurred.
- `changing reported`—contains data for instance-specific messages.

To summarize, the `get_instance_features` method enables you to check features for a list of instances using the parameters mentioned. The instances, features and results can be dynamically controlled by calling the method to perform various tests and actions in relation to the features of the entities.

In the following example, we are disabling the `update` and `delete` operations for entities with the status `N` (see Listing 5.15).

```
METHOD get_instance_features.
  SELECT *
    FROM z_i_travel
    FOR ALL ENTRIES IN @keys
    WHERE travelid = @keys-travelid
    INTO TABLE @DATA(lt_travels).

  result = VALUE #( FOR ls_travel IN lt_travels (
    travelid = ls_travel-travelid
    %features = SWITCH #( ls_travel-status
      WHEN 'N'
        THEN VALUE #(
          %delete = if_abap_behv=>fc-o-disabled
          %update = if_abap_behv=>fc-o-disabled
        )
      ELSE
        VALUE #(
          %delete = if_abap_behv=>fc-o-enabled
          %update = if_abap_behv=>fc-o-enabled
        )
    )
  ) ).
ENDMETHOD.
```

Listing 5.15: "get_instance_features" method

We start the Fiori preview again and select an instance that has travel status N. This is TRAVEL ID 5, as shown in Figure 5.25.

Figure 5.25: Feature control—UI

Due to the instance feature we implemented, the DELETE and EDIT buttons cannot be used on either the list page or the object page.

To summarize, in the RAP framework, feature control enables the dynamic control of the display and availability of data fields, operations, functions, and actions based on the status of a business object instance. This control can be both static and dynamic. In an instance-based context, dynamic feature control enables individual, runtime-controlled adaptation of access restrictions and display properties. Our example method `get_instance_features` demonstrated the implementation of a dynamic feature in which the operation is only activated when certain conditions are met. This flexible feature control helps to improve the user experience in SAP Fiori UI and makes it easier to adapt to business requirements.

5.7 Unmanaged save

RAP offers numerous built-in functionalities that enable developers to focus on actual business logic. While it handles many standard functionalities automatically, *unmanaged save* enables developers to take full control of BO's storage logic. This is particularly useful in cases where the standardized functionality of RAP is not sufficient. In these cases, developers have to manually implement all CRUD operations, which enables customization for specific business requirements, but at the same time involves much more responsibility and complexity.

5.7.1 General principles

In RAP, there are three different save scenarios for BO storage:

1. **Managed save** (standard)—in standard mode, saving takes place according to the rules of managed runtime. All changed instances of the BO entity are stored in the persistent table (DB_TABLE) in the database. The RAP framework takes care of the entire storage process, including the execution of determinations, validations, and actions defined for the specific entity.
2. **Managed save in conjunction with additional save**—this is basically a managed save, but developers can insert user-defined logic before or after the standard save. For example, additional actions may be required after a data record has been saved. After an employee data record has been saved, additional information can be saved via user-defined logic, or an onboarding workflow can be initiated for a new employee.
3. **Unmanaged save**—in this case, developers have greater control over the save process. This mode is particularly useful in scenarios where there are special requirements. This includes the freedom to implement custom data processing logic that goes beyond simple operations. For example, a complex business process might require a series of calculations before data has persisted. Developers can also decide to store data under certain conditions, or based on specific business logic.

Our focus here will be on unmanaged saves, and we will not go into additional save scenarios in detail.

For each BO entity, or for the entire BO, you can specify in the behavior definition whether the complete save process should be carried out by the managed runtime or by an unmanaged save procedure.

Unmanaged save can be relevant if we need to implement the interaction phase. For example, it could be that optimized program code already exists. In this case, the functions for the persistent saving of business data changes are called to save the data changes of the relevant BO entity. The managed runtime is overridden, and developers take responsibility for the saving process.

5.7.2 Definition and implementation

We will now look at the practical definition and implementation of unmanaged save in RESTful ABAP.

! Unmanaged save—persistent table not permitted

By adding unmanaged save, the automatic saving is switched off and the framework code that normally handles saving in the persistent table is no longer executed automatically. Therefore, we need to remove the previously added line `persistent table /DMO/TRAVEL` (see Section 3.2.2), because automatic save is deactivated. We now have to implement our own logic for saving. This gives us the freedom to design persistence logic according to our specific requirements and to implement individual saving processes for each entity.

Unmanaged save is part of the behavior definition. The statement can be made in two ways:

1. **In the body of the behavior definition**—`with unmanaged save` can be added to the behavior definition. This statement then applies to **all** entities. That is why this variant is also referred to as *compact notation*. The definition of behavior implementation can also be defined compactly (see Figure 5.26). Note the information above regarding the `persistent table`.

```
managed with unmanaged save implementation in class zcl_i_travel unique;
```

Figure 5.26: Unmanaged save—body of the behavior definition

2. **Entity-based**—a behavior definition can contain several entities. `Unmanaged save` can then only be activated for individual entities. To do this, add it to the `define behavior` clause of the entity to be activated (see Figure 5.27). Note again the information above about the `persistent table`.

```
define behavior for Z_I_TRAVEL //alias <alias_name>
//persistent table /DMO/TRAVEL
lock master
authorization master ( instance )
late numbering
with unmanaged save
{
```

Figure 5.27: Unmanaged save—entity-based

In our example, we apply variant 2 (entity-based) and extend the behavior clause of the *Z_I_TRAVEL* entity to include the unmanaged save functionality. To do this, we add the statement `with unmanaged save` and remove the statement `persistent table /DMO/TRAVEL`.

This leads to an inconsistency or an error in the behavior implementation class (see Figure 5.28:):

```
Class can't be analyzed during BDEF implementation check. Inconsistencies or errors exist: The BEHAVIOR method "SAVE_MODIFIED" must be redefined.
strict;
```

Figure 5.28: Inconsistent class after switching to unmanaged save

This inconsistency is because the `save_modified` method has already been implemented in the superclass by default. Activating unmanaged save results in managed save being deactivated. This then requires a redefinition of the managed-save method. To do this, we extend our behavior implementation class to include the method definition and implementation (see Figure 5.29).

```
CLASS lsc_z_i_travel DEFINITION INHERITING FROM cl_abap_behavior_saver.

  PROTECTED SECTION.

    METHODS save_modified REDEFINITION.

    METHODS adjust_numbers REDEFINITION.

ENDCLASS.

CLASS lsc_z_i_travel IMPLEMENTATION.

  METHOD save_modified.

  ENDMETHOD.
```

Figure 5.29: Method "save_modified"—redefined

The `save_modified` method is now the key component of the `unmanaged save` functionality, which is called every time the standard CUD (create, update, delete) operation is called.

Before we implement the method, let's look at its parameters in more detail (see Figure 5.30).

One import parameter (`create, update, delete`) is available for each standard operation. The import parameter's data type is `type request for change/delete`. It is a flat structure that contains the entities that have been marked as `unmanaged save` as an attribute in the structure; i.e., the operation can access the respective entity with import parameter and entity name (such as `create-z_i_travel`).

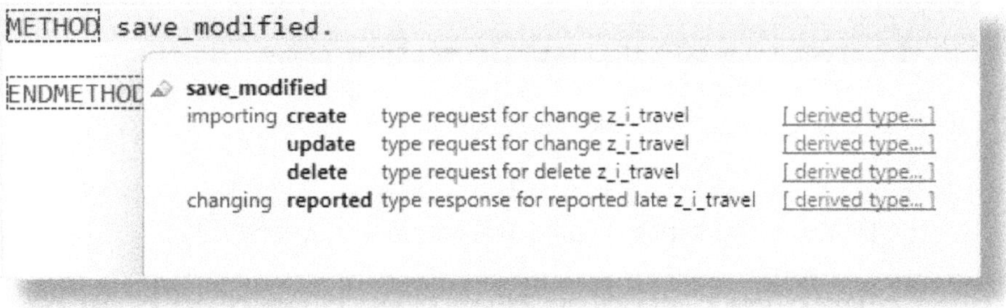

Figure 5.30: Method "save_modified"—parameters

The attribute in the structure is in turn a `type standard table` of the entity, including the `%control structure` (see Figure 5.31).

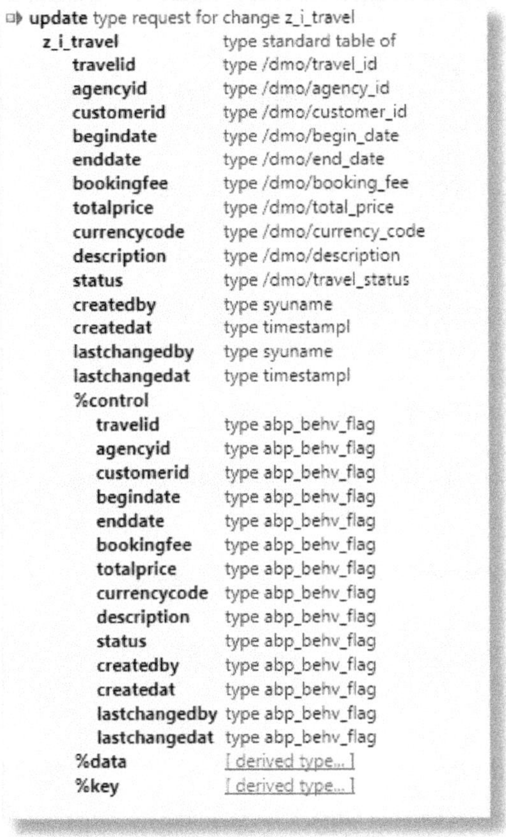

Figure 5.31: RAP data typ —"type request"

We will now focus on implementating the save_modified method (see Listing 5.16).

```
  METHOD save_modified.
    IF create IS NOT INITIAL. "Process create
      MODIFY /dmo/travel FROM TABLE @( CORRESPONDING #(
create-z_i_travel MAPPING FROM ENTITY ) ).

    ELSEIF update IS NOT INITIAL. "Process update
      TYPES tt_loc_rap_type LIKE update-z_i_travel.

      "Read local entity by EML
      READ ENTITIES OF z_i_travel IN LOCAL MODE
        ENTITY z_i_travel
        ALL FIELDS WITH CORRESPONDING #( update-z_i_travel )
        RESULT DATA(lt_travel_result)
        REPORTED DATA(lt_travel_reported)
        FAILED DATA(lt_travel_failed).

      IF lt_travel_failed IS INITIAL.
        DATA(lt_local_travels) = CORRESPONDING tt_loc_rap_
type( lt_travel_result ).
        "Update from local mapped entity
        MODIFY /dmo/travel FROM TABLE @( CORRESPONDING #(
lt_local_travels MAPPING FROM ENTITY ) ).
      ENDIF.

    ELSEIF delete IS NOT INITIAL. "Process delete
      DATA lr_travels_delete TYPE RANGE OF /dmo/travel-
travel_id.
      lr_travels_delete = VALUE #( FOR ls_travel_delete IN
delete-z_i_travel
         ( sign = 'I' option = 'EQ' low = ls_travel_delete-
travelid )
        ).
      DELETE FROM /dmo/travel WHERE travel_id IN @lr_
travels_delete.
    ENDIF.

  ENDMETHOD.
```

Listing 5.16: "save_modified" method

Let's examine the method step by step:

1. The method contains **conditional branches** to identify the various CUD operations performed during the current transaction: create, update, or delete.

2. **CREATE processing**:

   ▶ If the import variable `create` contains values, the branch for processing `create` is executed.

   ▶ The `MODIFY` statement is used to create data records in the `/dmo/travel` table. This involves `CORRESPONDING` with `MAPPING FROM ENTITY`.

3. **UPDATE processing:**

   ▶ If the import variable `update` contains values, the branch for processing `update` is executed.

   ▶ First, an attempt is made to read the local data of the entity `z_i_travel` using Entity Manipulation Language (EML) and to save the `RESULT` of the EML READ in `lt_travel_result`. In the case of an error, the EML parameters `FAILED` and `REPORTED` are filled in the corresponding structures. As the EML operation is made within its own BO, we deactivate the authorization check with the `IN LOCAL MODE` statement. If, on the other hand, the call originates from an ABAP program, for example, we should not use the `IN LOCAL MODE` statement — this would cause the program to terminate.

   ▶ If the read is successful (i.e., no errors occurred), the data is copied to `lt_local_travels`.

   ▶ A `MODIFY` is then performed for the `/dmo/travel` entity based on the locally read data.

4. **DELETE processing:**

   ▶ If the import variable `delete` contains values, the branch for processing `delete` is executed.

   ▶ A `RANGE` of variable `lr_travels_delete` is created to define the travel IDs to be deleted.

   ▶ The data records in the `/dmo/travel` table, whose travel IDs are in the defined range, are then deleted.

In summary, integration of the unmanaged save scenario in RAP gives developers the opportunity to design the persistence logic according to their individual requirements. However, this increased degree of freedom is accompanied by higher development costs.

5.8 Draft concept

The concept of *draft* is an innovative function in RAP that is particularly relevant in scenarios with complex transactions and long processing times. It offers the option of keeping entity changes in a temporary, non-persistent state until they are finally confirmed and saved. This function is crucial for creating user-friendly and robust applications, especially in scenarios in which data is entered over a longer period of time or in which several users are working on the same data at the same time.

In this section, we will examine the *draft* concept in detail, discuss how it works and the underlying logic, and show how it is implemented in RAP applications. We will start with a general introduction that explains the concept and its meaning in the context of the RAP framework. We will then look at the technical aspects and discuss how drafts are designed and managed in ABAP environments. We will pay particular attention to the challenges and best practices in implementing the concept. Through practical examples and detailed explanations, you will come to understand the many possibilities it offers developers to effectively design complex data-handling processes in ABAP applications.

5.8.1 General principles

The draft concept in RAP represents a key innovation in the development of modern enterprise applications, especially regarding the management of transactional data. It aims to reduce the complexity of data processing and improve the user experience by providing a flexible and robust approach to handling business data in an incomplete or provisional state.

Figure 5.32 illustrates the interaction between the draft concept and active instances within the framework of the draft concept in RAP.

At the center of this concept is the *draft instance*, a preliminary version of a data set in which users make their changes. It represents a working draft that is saved in the *draft table*. This separation ensures that work being done on data has no direct impact on ongoing business processes.

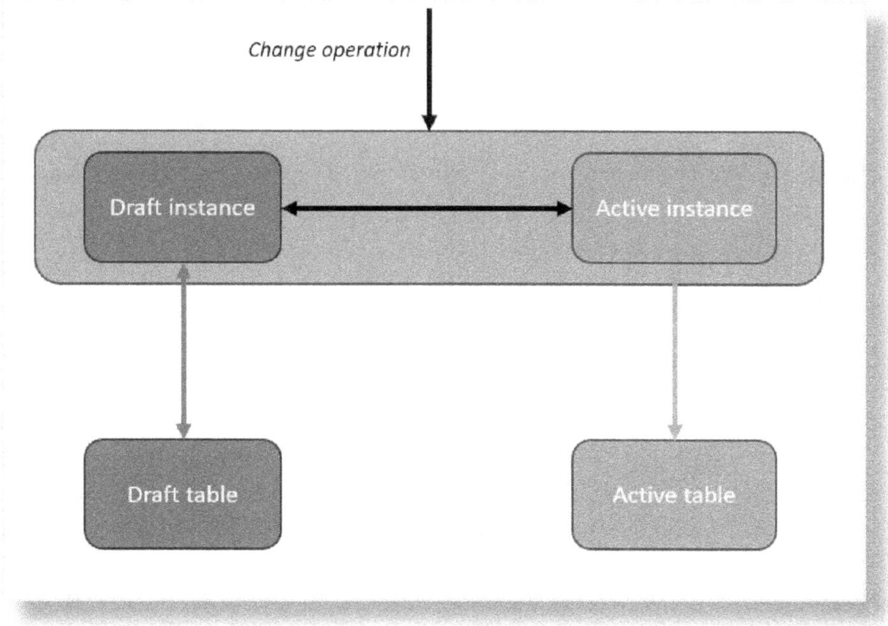

Figure 5.32: Draft concept

After a user has completed editing, the *draft instance* is converted into an *active instance*. This instance represents the binding status of the data, which is recorded in the *active table*. In this final table, the data is available for regular business operations and for further transactions.

The main features and advantages of drafting are as follows:

- **Separation of draft and active data**—a key component of the concept is the separate storage of draft data in shadow tables (draft tables). This separation preserves the integrity of the active data and ensures that the draft data does not impair regular operation and data quality.
- **Improved user experience**—the concept makes a significant contribution to user-friendliness. Users can seamlessly start, interrupt, and resume work steps at a later time. This is particularly beneficial in complex business applications where processing can take a long time.
- **Integration into the RAP framework**—the draft concept is deeply integrated into the RAP framework. This enables automated management of draft data, which considerably simplifies the development process.

- **Improved error handling and data validation**—before the data is transferred to active state, the draft concept enables thorough error handling and data validation. This contributes to increased data quality and security.

The above explanations provide a comprehensive overview of the general foundation of the draft concept, which significantly improves the efficiency, integrity and user-friendliness of RAP. The following section focuses on practical implementation, based on an understanding of the underlying principles and structures.

5.8.2 Implementation

As an example, we will add the draft concept to the existing application. This means that all changes are automatically saved temporarily while editing until they are finally persisted in the database. In Section 5.7 we implemented an unmanaged save. For the remainder of this book, we will deactivate the unmanaged save functionality, because the draft functionality requires a `persistent table`.

To implement the draft concept, it is necessary to adjust the behavior definition `Z_I_TRAVEL` (see Listing 5.17). To do this, we open the behavior definition. As shown in the listing, the previously mentioned deconstruction of the unmanaged save functionality has been carried out.

```
managed implementation in class zcl_i_travel unique;
strict;
with draft;

define behavior for Z_I_TRAVEL //alias <alias_name>
persistent table /DMO/TRAVEL
draft table zdmo_travel_d
lock master
total etag Lastchangedat
authorization master ( instance )
late numbering
//with unmanaged save
{
  create;
  update (features : instance);
  delete (features : instance);
```

```
   field (readonly) TravelId;

   determination setDefaultBeginDate on modify { create; }
   validation checkCurrency on save { field CurrencyCode; }
   static action cancelTravel parameter Z_A_CANCEL_TRAVEL;
   function countTravel result [1..*] $self;

   draft action Resume ;
   draft action Activate ;
   draft action Edit ;
   draft action Discard ;
   draft determine action Prepare  {
     validation checkCurrency;
   }


   mapping for /dmo/travel
   {
     TravelId = travel_id;
     AgencyId = agency_id;
     BeginDate = begin_date;
     BookingFee = booking_fee;
     Createdat = createdat;
     Createdby = createdby;
     CurrencyCode = currency_code;
     CustomerId = customer_id;
     Description = description;
     EndDate = end_date;
     Lastchangedat = lastchangedat;
     Lastchangedby = lastchangedby;
     Status = status;
     TotalPrice = total_price;
   }
 }
```

Listing 5.17: Implementing the draft concept—behavior definition "Z_I_TRAVEL"

In changing the behavior definition, we have activated the drafting feature using the command `with draft;`. We also specified the name of the draft table (`draft table zdmo_travel_d`) and the ETag attribute (`total etag Lastchangedat`). We then added the draft actions to the list of operations.

After updating the code in the behavior definition, errors are displayed because there is no draft table yet. To create one, we can use the quick-fix function. This is used to automatically generate the table `zdmo_travel_d`. If no quick-fix option is offered, click on the table name and press key combination `Ctrl` + `1`. The function CREATE DRAFT TABLE ZDMO_TRAVEL_D FOR ENTITY Z_I_TRAVEL can then be executed by double-clicking on it (see Figure 5.33).

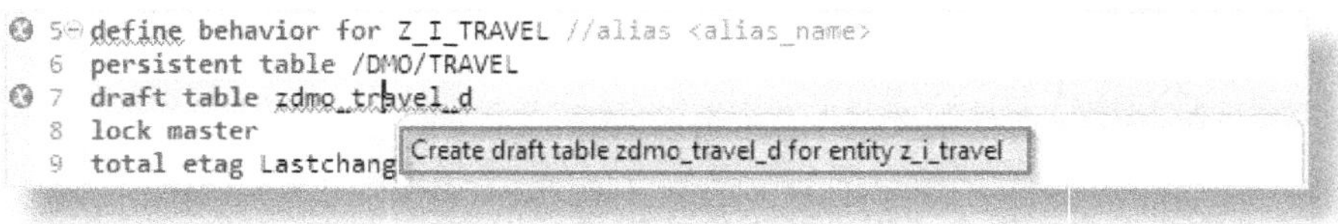

Figure 5.33: Creating draft table—getting started

In the next step, the NEW DRAFT TABLE window opens, which is used to create the new shadow table (see Figure 5.34). Because the NAME and DESCRIPTION of the new object are automatically preset, we now just click the NEXT ❶ button to continue with the creation.

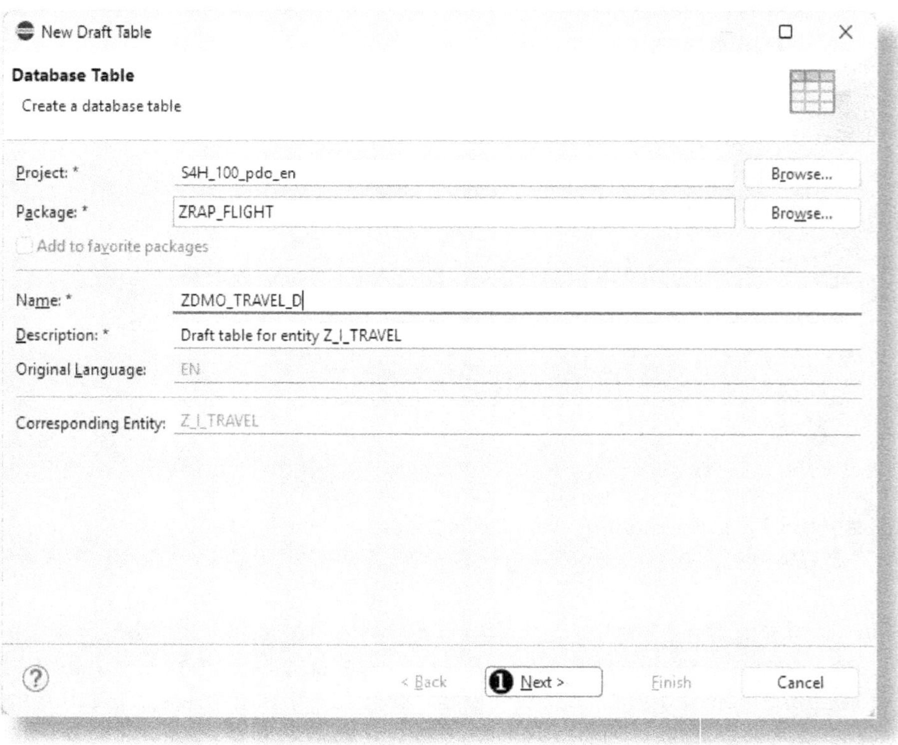

Figure 5.34: Creating draft table —dialog

We are then taken to the next screen, where we specify a transport. We end by clicking on FINISH.

The newly created draft table then opens (see Listing 5.18).

```
@EndUserText.label : 'Draft table for entity Z_I_TRAVEL'
@AbapCatalog.enhancement.category : #EXTENSIBLE_ANY
@AbapCatalog.tableCategory : #TRANSPARENT
@AbapCatalog.deliveryClass : #A
@AbapCatalog.dataMaintenance : #RESTRICTED
define table zdmo_travel_d {

  key mandt      : mandt not null;
  key travelid   : /dmo/travel_id not null;
  key draftuuid  : sdraft_uuid not null;
  agencyid       : /dmo/agency_id;
  customerid     : /dmo/customer_id;
  begindate      : /dmo/begin_date;
  enddate        : /dmo/end_date;
  @Semantics.amount.currencyCode : 'zdmo_travel_d.
currencycode'
  bookingfee     : /dmo/booking_fee;
  @Semantics.amount.currencyCode : 'zdmo_travel_d.
currencycode'
  totalprice     : /dmo/total_price;
  currencycode   : /dmo/currency_code;
  description    : /dmo/description;
  status         : /dmo/travel_status;
  createdby      : syuname;
  createdat      : timestampl;
  lastchangedby  : syuname;
  lastchangedat  : timestampl;
  "%admin"       : include sych_bdl_draft_admin_inc;
}
```

Listing 5.18: Draft table "ZDMO_TRAVEL_D"

We activate the table using the button. As soon as the table is activated, we switch back to our behavior definition `Z_I_TRAVEL`, which is also activated via the button.

In the last step, we need to remove the `save_modified` method in our behavior implementation class *ZCL_I_TRAVEL*. To do this, delete the method definition and its implementation (see Figure 5.35).

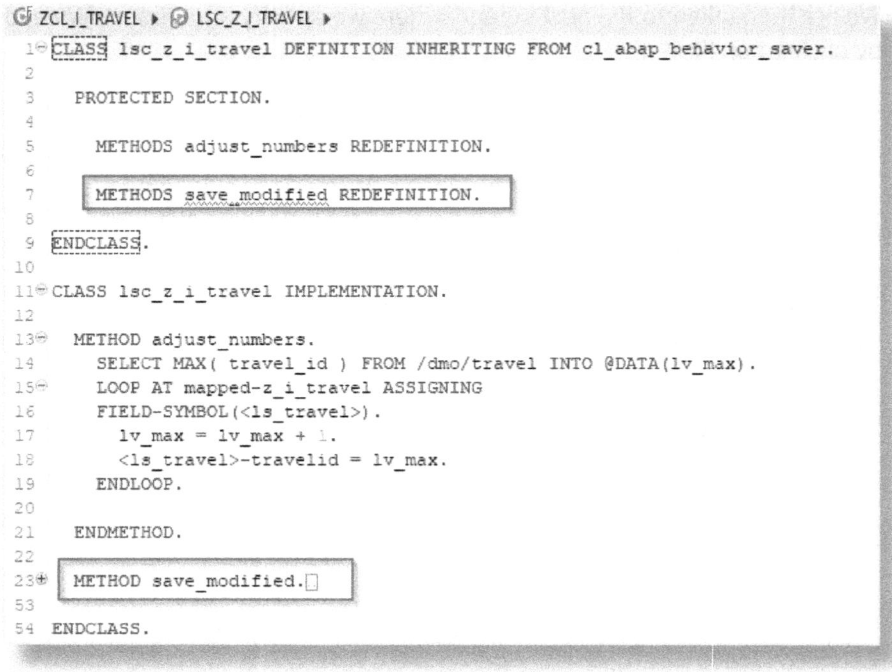

Figure 5.35: Deleting the save_modified method

Subsequent activation, via the button, saves the changes to the class and activates them.

The inclusion of a draft at the interface level is complete. We now turn our attention to extending the consumption level. To do this, open the consumption behavior definition `Z_C_TRAVEL` and add the lines highlighted in Listing 5.19.

```
projection;
strict;
use draft;

define behavior for Z_C_TRAVEL //alias <alias_name>
{
  use create;
  use update;
  use delete;

  use action cancelTravel;
  use function countTravel;
```

```
    use action Edit;
    use action Activate;
    use action Discard;
    use action Prepare;
    use action Resume;

  }
```

Listing 5.19: Draft behavior definition "Z_C_TRAVEL"

In changing the projection behavior definition, we have activated the drafting feature (`use draft;`) and included the draft actions.

In the following step, we test the new development in the preview. To do this, we navigate to our previously created service binding Z_TRAVEL_SB_V2 and press the PREVIEW... button (see Figure 5.36).

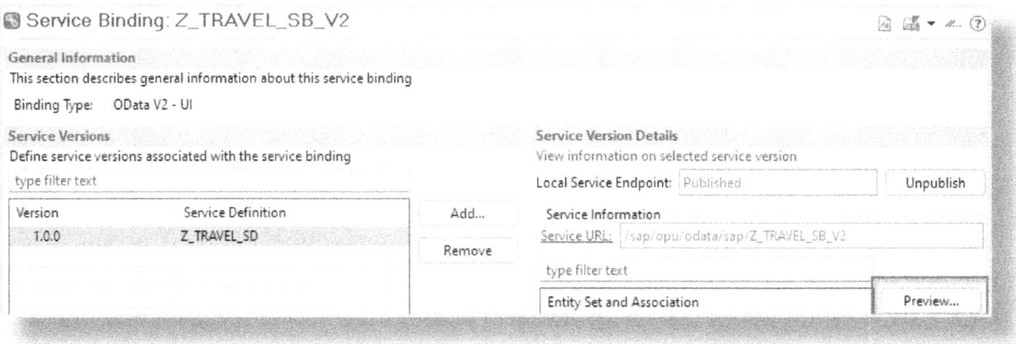

Figure 5.36: Fiori "Preview" button

The Fiori application preview now opens (see Figure 5.37).

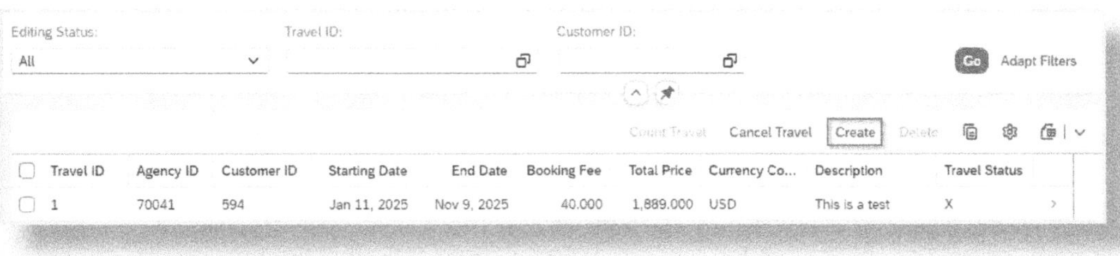

Figure 5.37: Fiori application

At first glance, no changes are noticeable.

To demonstrate the draft function, we create a new travel by clicking on the CREATE button. We are then taken to the object page where we create a new travel. We enter random values for the various attributes of the travel (see Figure 5.38).

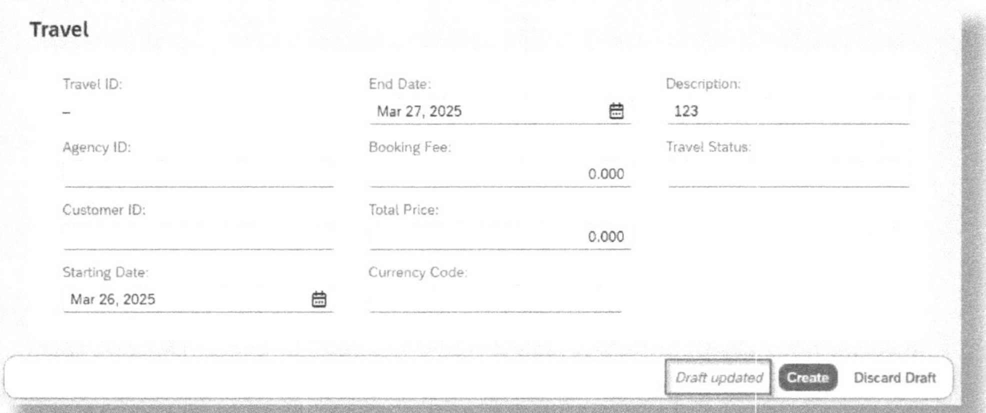

Figure 5.38: Creating travel draft

Note that when inputting data or leaving the input fields blank, the DRAFT UPDATED display at the bottom of the window indicates that the draft object has been saved—the temporary object is saved in the draft table.

The draft table ZDMO_TRAVEL_D—either via transaction *SE16(N)* or via data preview in Eclipse—shows that a fresh entry has been created for the newly created travel (see Figure 5.39).

Click on the CREATE button on the object page and this temporary entry is removed from the shadow table, this initiates the process of transferring the data to the main table `/DMO/TRAVEL` (i.e., its persistence).

If we now try to leave this object page without creating the travel, a pop-up window appears informing us that a draft of the travel exists. Normally, the object page for creating is closed via the back button (<)_at the top left (see Figure 5.40). However, after we click on it, a message is displayed, with several options:

- KEEP DRAFT—we can keep the draft object.
- DISCARD DRAFT—we can delete the draft object.
- CANCEL—we can stay on the current screen.

Fld Name	Value
Client	100
Travel Number	00000000
Draft Document (Technical ID)	733EFE7953E61FE082C94B28D90DF...
Agency Number	000000
Customer Number	000000
Starting Date	26.03.2025
End Date	27.03.2025
Booking Fee	0,00
Total Price	0,00
Currency Code	
Description	123
Travel Status	
User Name	
Time Stamp	00.00.0000 00:00:00
User Name	
Time Stamp	00.00.0000 00:00:00
Created On	26.03.2025 13:58:09
Last Changed On	26.03.2025 13:58:48
UUID	733EFE7953E61FE082C94B28D90E1...
Draft - Operation Code	C
Has active instance	
Field Changes	0000000101010100010000000000FF..
Number of Entries	0

Figure 5.39: Transaction "SE16N" —draft table

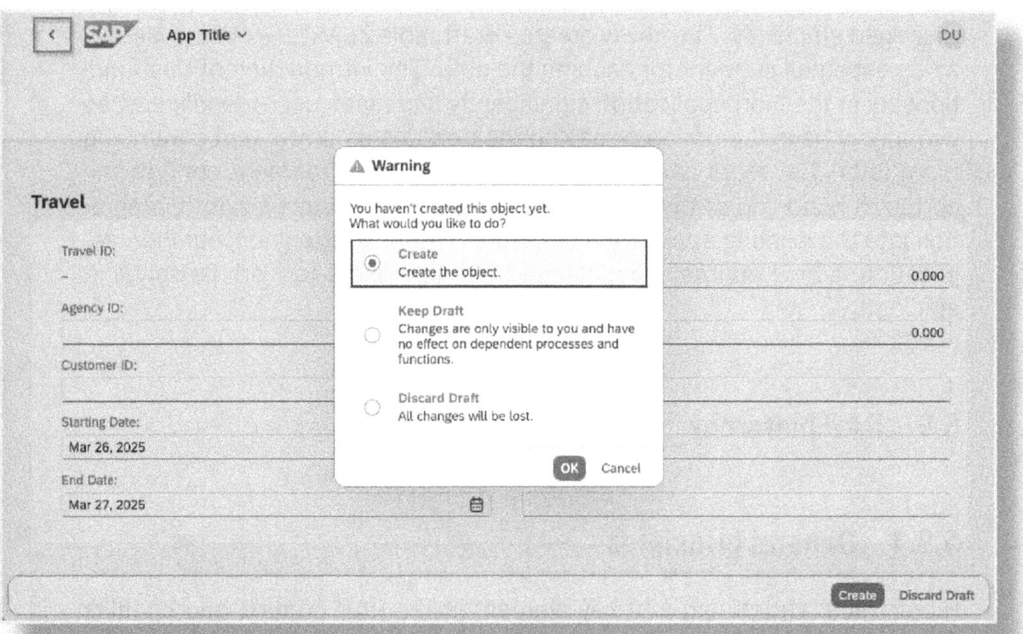

Figure 5.40: Exiting object page

In addition to the back button, there are also other ways to exit the screen, for example via DISCARD DRAFT at the bottom right. Here, too, we are asked whether we want to keep or delete the draft object. However, if we close the browser tab, no pop-up appears. If we open the Fiori application again later, we will find the draft object at the top of the list, with a blue vertical line to the left, clearly marking it as a draft (see Figure 5.41). This enables us to continue editing seamlessly.

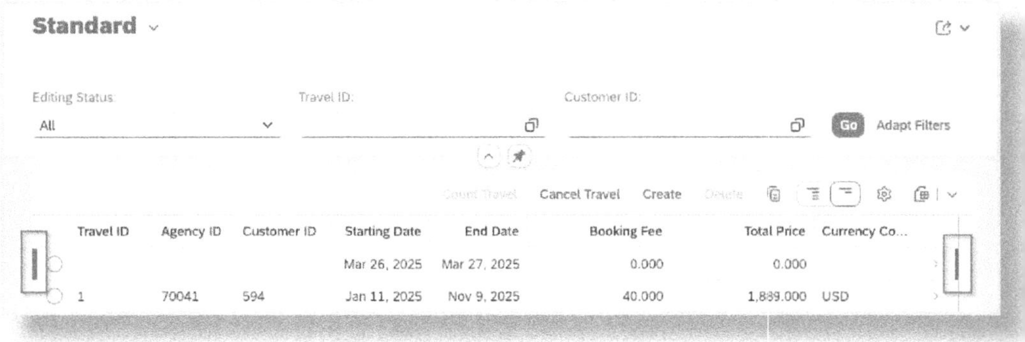

Figure 5.41: List with draft object

We have now successfully completed the implementation of the draft concept for the Fiori application. The adjustments made to the behavior definitions at both interface and consumption level now enable drafts to be managed efficiently. The newly created draft table *ZDMO_TRAVEL_D* serves as an essential element for caching the data. The introduction of this functionality in the Fiori application significantly increases user-friendliness, as users now have the option of saving their entries as drafts and continuing them later. The tests carried out in the preview environment confirm the correct functioning of the draft feature and demonstrate a smooth integration into the existing application structure. With this extension, our Fiori application is now optimally positioned to enable users to work flexibly and efficiently.

5.9 RAP hierarchy

5.9.1 General principles

Hierarchical structuring is a key element in the RAP context and enables developers to extend the functions of existing BOs by adding new entities or nodes. Each new node has its own data model, which is integrated into the existing data model as a link entity. Emphasis is placed on the creation of a hierarchical order, whereby *parent-child relationships* are at the center. The parent entity, which is defined as the *root view entity*, forms the basis of the hierarchy, while the child entities (*view entities*) represent the extended nodes. The behavior for a child entity is defined in the parent behavior definition, followed by an extension of the service definition to make the new node visible.

The following points highlight the fundamental aspects of the hierarchical component, its architectural principles, and the underlying philosophy:

- **Definition of the new child node**—by introducing a new node, the extension of a RAP-BO enriches the existing data model with additional nodes. These nodes significantly increase the flexibility and adaptability of the BO. The new node represents a child entity that is located directly below the parent entity.
- **Architecture of the new child node**—the architecture of the new node is based on the clear definition of the relationships between the nodes and the existing BO data model. A crucial aspect is the establishment of a *to-parent relationship* that defines the hierarchy between the new child nodes and the parent entity of the data model.
- **Data model of the child node**—an independent data model of the child node is required for the node link. This is integrated into the existing data model as a child entity and contains the necessary information and attributes. To ensure seamless integration, the hierarchy and relationships are carefully modeled.
- **Behavior for the new node**—the behavior definition and implementation of the child node is defined and included in the behavior of the parent entity. This defines how the new node interacts with other parts of the BO, which operations it supports, and which authorizations and locks apply. The clear definition of create, update, and delete operations plays a central role in ensuring the integrity of the BO.
- **Integration into the service**—in addition to integration in the data model and in the behavior, the node is also integrated into the OData service. By extending the service definition, the new node is exposed in the service so that external applications can access the extended functions.

Overall, the hierarchical component enables flexible adaptation and optimization of existing RAP-BOs, which significantly promotes agility in application development.

5.9.2 Implementation

As an example, we will create a bidirectional hierarchical link between the travels and the bookings (see Figure 5.42).

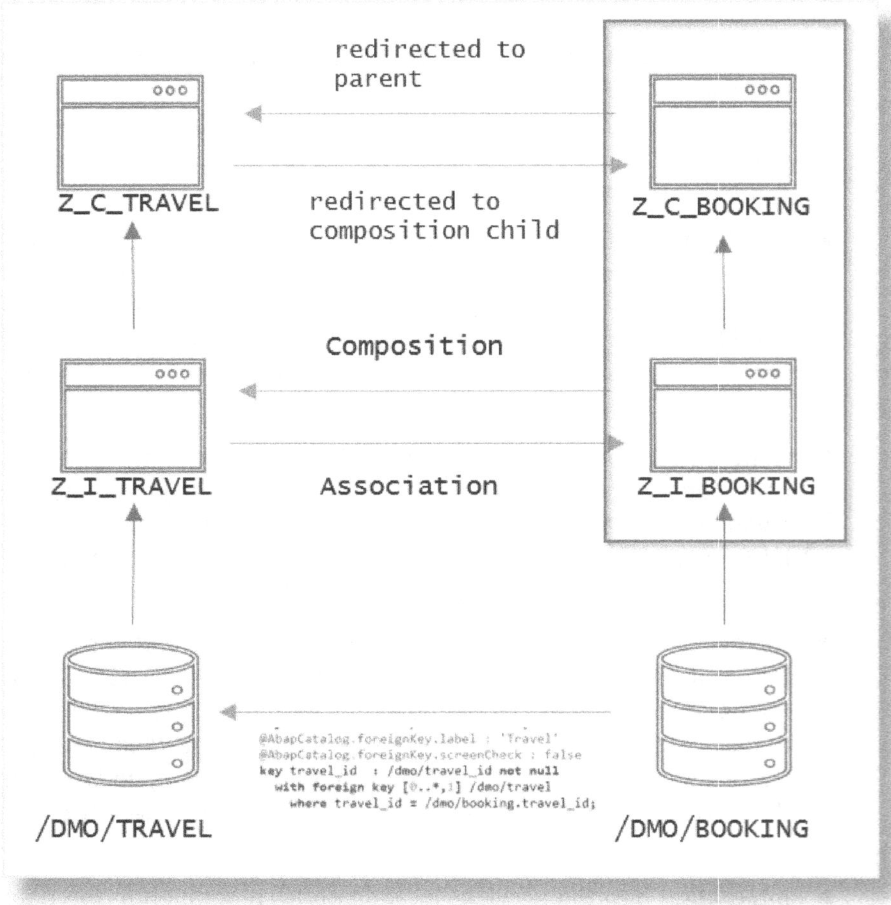

Figure 5.42: Architecture—hierarchy

Put simply, no booking can be created without an existing travel. Such an architecture guarantees that each booking instance is inextricably linked to a specific travel instance.

The components `Z_I_BOOKING` (interface) and `Z_C_BOOKING` (consumption) are new objects that need to be created. These are normal CDS view entities, not root view entities.

View entity

In RAP, a *root view entity* is the central entry point of a BO, which is responsible for the main data structure and the execution of CRUD operations. In contrast, normal, or non-root, view entities supplement the BO with detailed or specific data structures, but do not perform any independent CRUD operations. While the root view entity controls the core functionalities and key attributes of the BO, normal view entities are used to structure and extend the overall model.

The database table */DMO/BOOKING*, which is supplied in the standard package of the flight reference model, is used for bookings. This table has a 1:n relationship with the */DMO/TRAVEL* table; i.e., a travel can contain n bookings. Based on this relational data model, we will create the complementary model in RAP and display it visually in a Fiori application.

First, we create the interface view *Z_I_BOOKING* and create a composition relationship with the root view *Z_I_TRAVEL*. We also need to create an association relationship between *Z_I_BOOKING* and *Z_I_TRAVEL*. In our package *ZRAP_FLIGHT*, we right-click on DATA DEFINITIONS ❶ and select the menu item NEW DATA DEFINITION ❷ (see Figure 5.43).

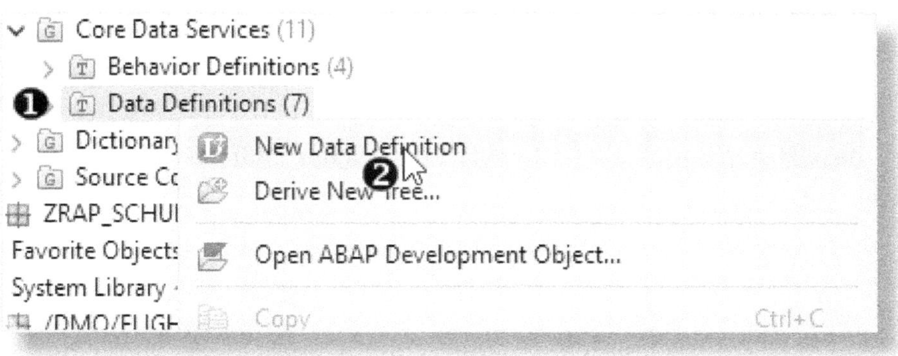

Figure 5.43: Appendix "Z_I_BOOKING" – Getting started

The NEW DATA DEFINITION creation window appears (see Figure 5.44), where we enter the NAME *Z_I_BOOKING* ❶ and the DESCRIPTION *Interface View Booking* ❷. We continue by clicking on the NEXT button ❸.

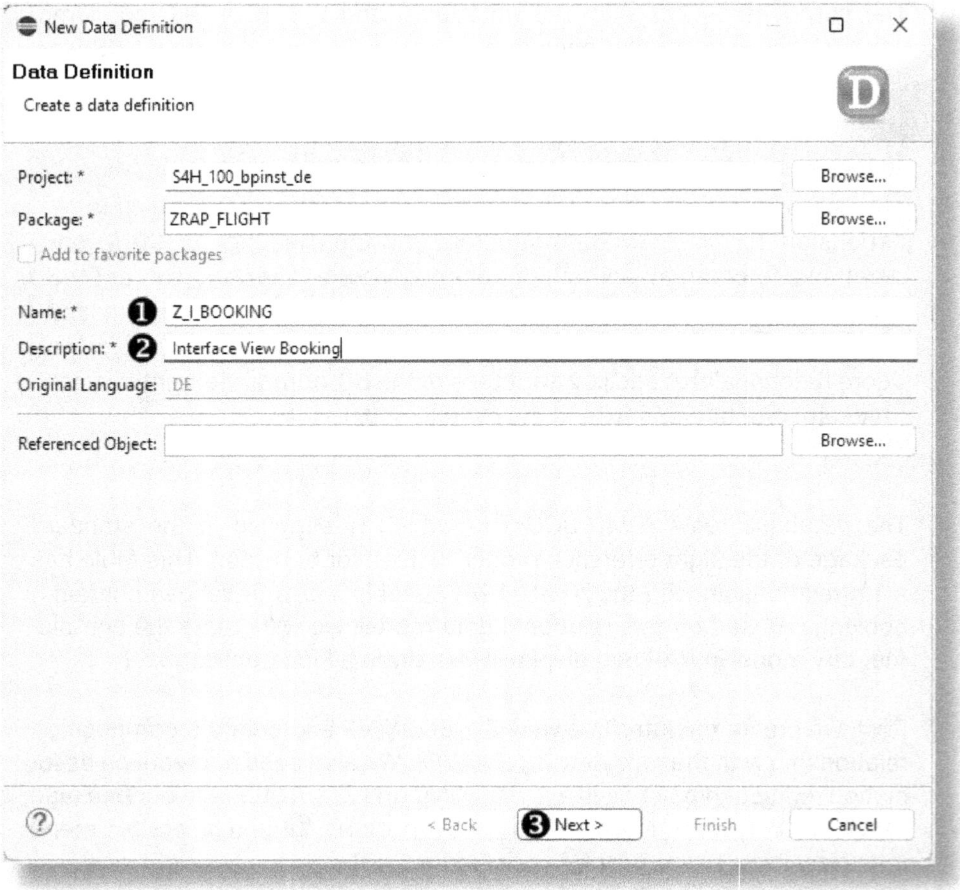

Figure 5.44: Appendix "Z_I_BOOKING"—next screen

Select a transport and confirm again by clicking on NEXT.

The next step is to select the template (see Figure 5.45). Select DEFINE VIEW ENTITY ❶ and complete the creation by clicking on the FINISH button ❷.

The CDS editor then opens. The code for the new CDS entity can be found in Listing 5.20.

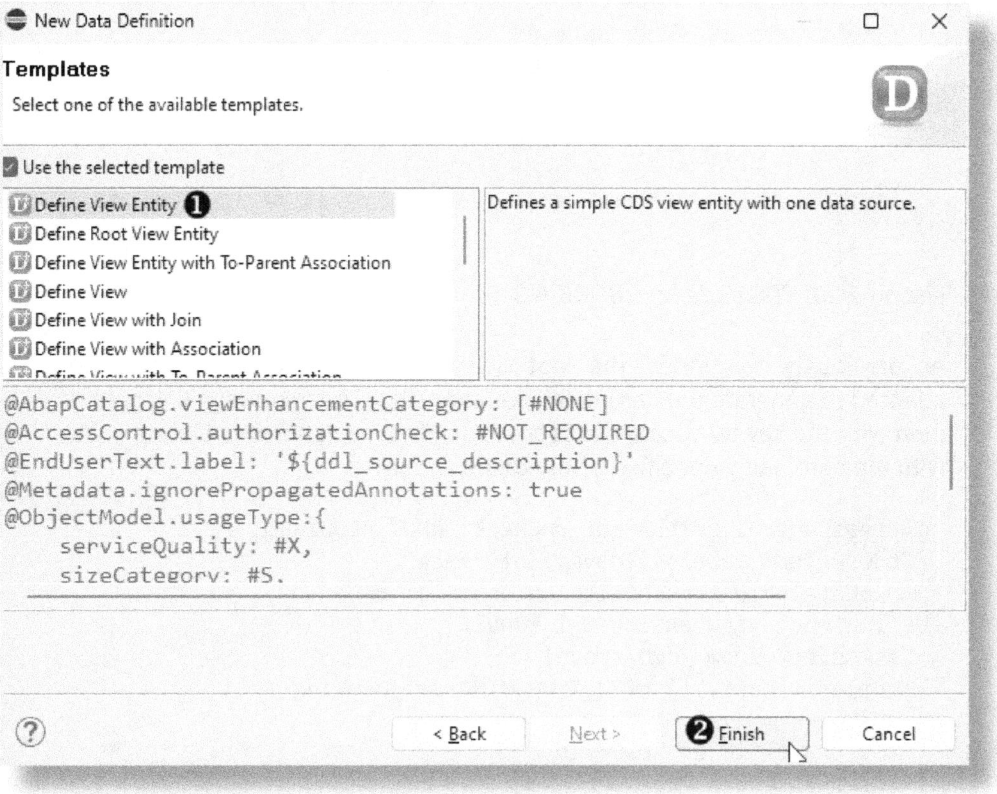

Figure 5.45: Creating "Z_I_BOOKING"—selecting the template

```
@AccessControl.authorizationCheck: #NOT_REQUIRED
@EndUserText.label: 'Interface View Booking'
define view entity Z_I_BOOKING as select from /dmo/booking
  association to parent Z_I_TRAVEL as _Travel on
$projection.TravelId = _Travel.TravelId
{
  key travel_id as TravelId,
  key booking_id as BookingId,
  booking_date as BookingDate,
  customer_id as CustomerId,
  carrier_id as CarrierId,
  connection_id as ConnectionId,
```

```
   flight_date as FlightDate,
   @Semantics.amount.currencyCode: 'CurrencyCode'
   flight_price as FlightPrice,
   currency_code as CurrencyCode,

   _Travel
}
```

Listing 5.20: CDS code "Z_I_BOOKING"

As previously mentioned, the root view entity *Z_I_TRAVEL* needs to be adapted to generate the parent-child relationship. The relationship is generated with the key term `composition [1..*] of`, as shown in Listing 5.21, with the cardinality specified after `composition`.

```
@AccessControl.authorizationCheck: #NOT_REQUIRED
@EndUserText.label: 'Travel Interface'
@AbapCatalog.extensibility.extensible: true
define root view entity Z_I_TRAVEL
   as select from /dmo/travel
   composition[1..*] of Z_I_BOOKING as _Booking
{
   key travel_id as TravelId,
[ . . . ]
   _Booking
}
```

Listing 5.21: Adaptation "Z_I_TRAVEL"

In this example, `[1..*]` has been selected, meaning 1:n relationship. We then add the composition `_Booking` to the selection list.

The booking entity is now included in the travel root data model. A normal view entity does not have its own behavior definition and implementation.

We now open the existing behavior definition of the root entity travel (`Z_I_TRAVEL`) and define a block (sub-behavior) for the new child entity booking (`Z_I_BOOKING`). The sub-behavior is defined with the key words `define behavior` under the existing travel behavior (see Listing 5.22). We also need to include the booking entity with the keyword `association` as an association in the travel behavior.

```
managed implementation in class zcl_i_travel unique;
strict;
with draft;

define behavior for Z_I_TRAVEL //alias <alias_name>
persistent table /DMO/TRAVEL
draft table zdmo_travel_d
lock master
total etag Lastchangedat
authorization master ( instance )
late numbering
//with unmanaged save
{
[ . . . ]
  association _Booking {create; with draft; }
[ . . . ]
}

define behavior for Z_I_BOOKING //alias <alias_name>
persistent table /dmo/booking
draft table zdmo_booking_d
lock dependent
late numbering
authorization dependent {
  field (readonly) TravelId, BookingId;
  update;
  delete;
  association _Travel { with draft; }

  mapping for /DMO/BOOKING
  {
    TravelId = travel_id;
    BookingId = booking_id;
    BookingDate = booking_date;
    CustomerId = customer_id;
    CarrierId = carrier_id;
    ConnectionId = connection_id;
    FlightDate = flight_date;
    FlightPrice = flight_price;
    CurrencyCode = currency_code;
  }
}
```

Listing 5.22: Behavior definition "Z_I_TRAVEL" —adaptation

After adjusting the behavior definition, an error occurs because the draft table `zdmo_booking_d` specified there does not yet exist. A quick fix option appears, which guides us through the process of creating the table so that we can guarantee consistency in our definition.

Click on the quick fix icon and select menu item CREATE DRAFT TABLE ZDMO_BOOKING_D FOR ENTITY Z_I_BOOKING (see Figure 5.46).

Figure 5.46: Draft table—quick fix

In the next step, the NEW DRAFT TABLE window opens, where we create the new shadow table. The NAME and DESCRIPTION of the new object are automatically preset. To continue with the creation, click on the NEXT button ❶ (see Figure 5.47).

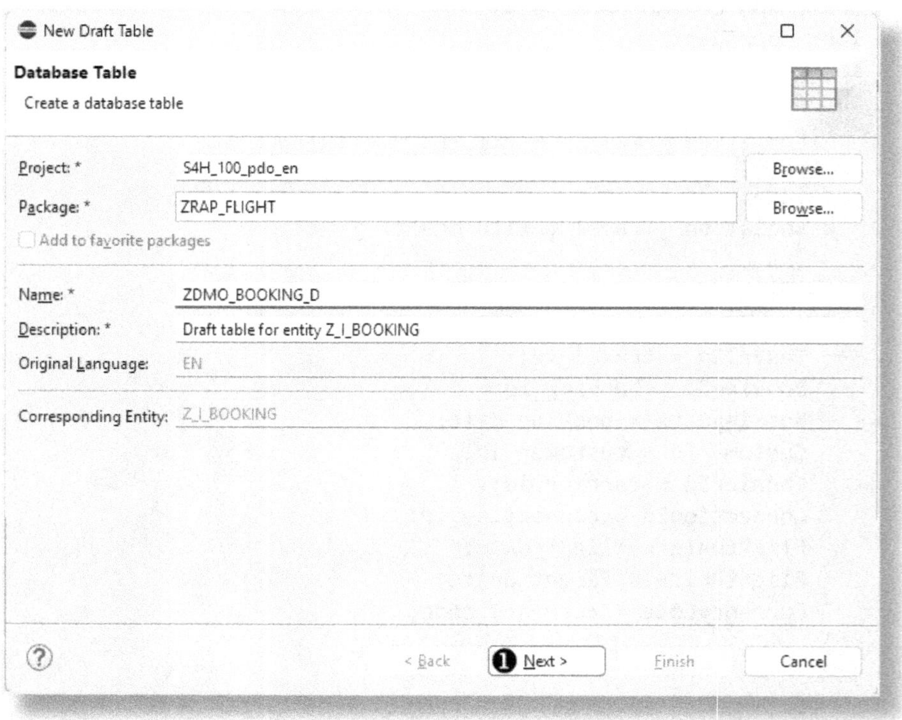

Figure 5.47: Creating draft table "Booking"

On the next screen, we need to specify a transport and end the activity by clicking on FINISH.

The newly created draft table—ZDMO_BOOKING_D—then opens (see Listing 5.23).

```
@EndUserText.label : 'Draft table for entity Z_I_BOOKING'
@AbapCatalog.enhancement.category : #EXTENSIBLE_ANY
@AbapCatalog.tableCategory : #TRANSPARENT
@AbapCatalog.deliveryClass : #A
@AbapCatalog.dataMaintenance : #RESTRICTED
define table zdmo_booking_d {

  key mandt         : mandt not null;
  key travelid      : /dmo/travel_id not null;
  key bookingid     : /dmo/booking_id not null;
  key draftuuid     : sdraft_uuid not null;
  parentdraftuuid   : sdraft_uuid;
  bookingdate       : /dmo/booking_date;
  customerid        : /dmo/customer_id;
  carrierid         : /dmo/carrier_id;
  connectionid      : /dmo/connection_id;
  flightdate        : /dmo/flight_date;
  @Semantics.amount.currencyCode : 'zdmo_booking_d.
currencycode'
  flightprice       : /dmo/flight_price;
  currencycode      : /dmo/currency_code;
  "%admin"          : include sych_bdl_draft_admin_inc;

}
```

Listing 5.23: Draft table "ZDMO_BOOKING_D"

In the next step, we switch back to the behavior definition `Z_I_TRAVEL` and activate the object via the button.

The `_Booking` association has been included in the travel behavior clause, meaning that a booking must be created via a travel. In contrast to independent entities that can be created directly, the creation of a booking instance requires navigation through the parent relationship. The close link promotes a clear structure and preserves data integrity.

The *late numbering* functionality has been defined for the main entity, and this must also be activated and implemented on the child entity. With late numbering, we can assign the booking ID upon creation. In the behavior implementation class *ZCL_I_TRAVEL* we extend the already created method `adjust_numbers`. The adapted code is shown in Listing 5.24.

```
METHOD adjust_numbers.
    SELECT MAX( travel_id ) FROM /dmo/travel INTO @DATA(lv_
max).

    LOOP AT mapped-z_i_travel ASSIGNING FIELD-SYMBOL(<ls_
travel>).
      lv_max = lv_max + 1.
      <ls_travel>-travelid = lv_max.
    ENDLOOP.

    DATA(lv_booking_index) = 1.
    LOOP AT mapped-z_i_booking ASSIGNING FIELD-SYMBOL(<ls_
booking>).
      DATA(ls_travel) = VALUE #( mapped-z_i_travel[ 1 ]
OPTIONAL ).

      IF ls_travel IS INITIAL.
        SELECT MAX( booking_id ) FROM /dmo/booking WHERE
travel_id = @<ls_booking>-%tmp-travelid INTO @DATA(lv_
max_b).
        lv_max_b = lv_max_b + lv_booking_index.
        <ls_booking>-bookingid = lv_max_b.
      ELSE.
        <ls_booking>-bookingid = lv_booking_index.
      ENDIF.
      <ls_booking>-travelid = <ls_booking>-%tmp-travelid.
      lv_booking_index += lv_booking_index.
    ENDLOOP.

ENDMETHOD.
```

Listing 5.24: Extended method "adjust_numbers"

This completes the addition of the booking entity or booking node at interface level. We will now turn our attention to enriching the consumption level. This requires the following steps:

1. New creation of the projection view *Z_C_BOOKING*, including to-parent relationship to *Z_C_TRAVEL* and UI annotations for display in the Fiori application.
2. Composition extension in *Z_C_TRAVEL* to *Z_C_BOOKING*, integration of the UI facet annotation to see the nodes on the object page of the travel.
3. Adaptation of the behavior definition *Z_C_TRAVEL*; i.e., inclusion of the child association in the root clause, and redefinition of the behavior for *Z_C_BOOKING*.

First, we create the new consumption view *Z_C_BOOKING*. In the project explorer (see Figure 5.48), we right-click on DATA DEFINITIONS ❶ and navigate to the menu item NEW DATA DEFINITION ❷.

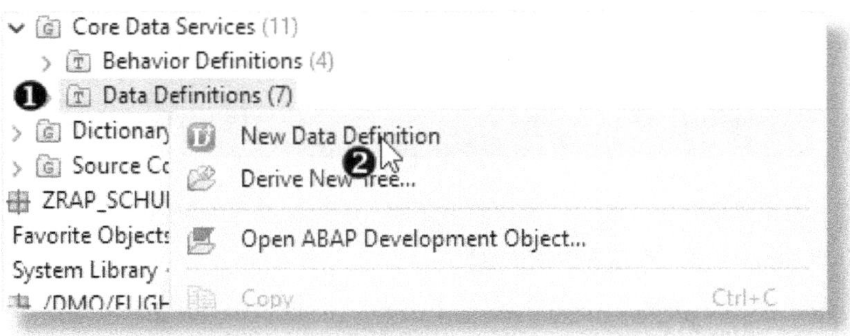

Figure 5.48: Creating a new data definition

The NEW DATA DEFINITION creation window appears (see Figure 5.49), where we select the NAME *Z_C_BOOKING* ❶ and the DESCRIPTION *Projection View Booking* ❷. We continue with the creation by clicking on the NEXT button ❸.

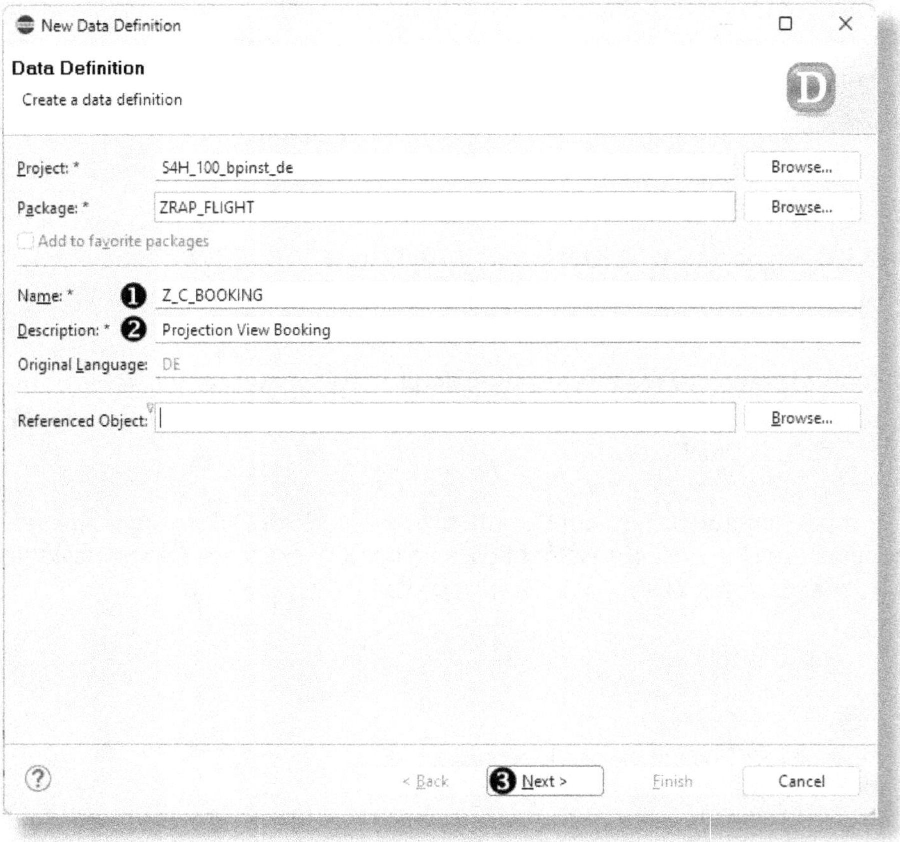

Figure 5.49: Appendix "Z_C_BOOKING"

A transport is selected and the NEXT button clicked again.

The selection of the template appears in the next step—we select the DEFINE PROJECTION VIEW ❶ template and finish by clicking on the FINISH ❷ button (see Figure 5.50).

The CDS editor then opens. The code for the new CDS entity can be found in Listing 5.25.

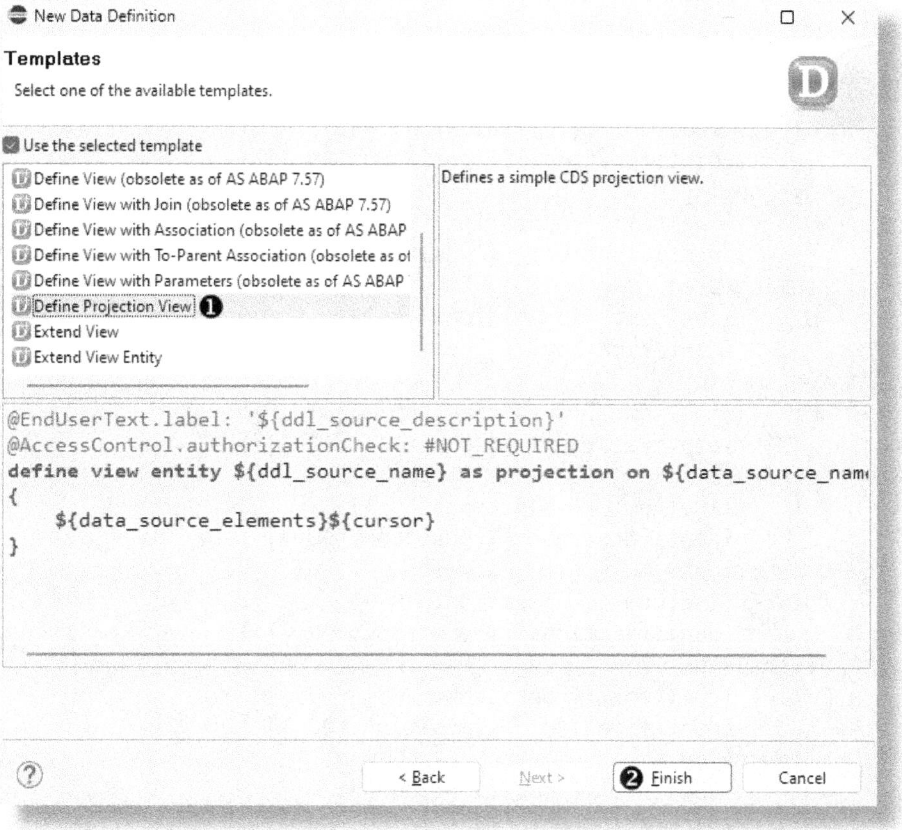

Figure 5.50: Select template

```
@EndUserText.label: 'Consumption View Booking'
@AccessControl.authorizationCheck: #NOT_REQUIRED
define view entity Z_C_BOOKING
  as projection on Z_I_BOOKING
{
  @UI.facet: [ {
    id: 'idIdentificationBooking',
    type: #IDENTIFICATION_REFERENCE,
    label: 'Booking',
    position: 10
  } ]
```

```
  @UI: { lineItem: [{ position: 10 }],
         identification: [{ position: 10 }] }
  key TravelId,
  @UI: { lineItem: [{ position: 20 }],
         identification: [{ position: 20 }] }
  key BookingId,
  @UI: { lineItem: [{ position: 30 }],
         identification: [{ position: 30 }] }
  BookingDate,
  @UI: { lineItem: [{ position: 40 }],
         identification: [{ position: 40 }] }
  CustomerId,
  @UI: { lineItem: [{ position: 50 }],
         identification: [{ position: 50 }] }
  CarrierId,
  @UI: { lineItem: [{ position: 60 }],
         identification: [{ position: 60 }] }
  ConnectionId,
  @UI: { lineItem: [{ position: 70 }],
         identification: [{ position: 70 }] }
  FlightDate,
  @UI: { lineItem: [{ position: 80 }],
         identification: [{ position: 80 }] }
  FlightPrice,
  @UI: { lineItem: [{ position: 90 }],
         identification: [{ position: 90 }] }
  CurrencyCode,
  /* Associations */
  _Travel: redirected to parent Z_C_TRAVEL
}
```

Listing 5.25: Consumption view "Z_C_BOOKING"

We now need to adapt the consumption root view entity *Z_C_TRAVEL* to create the composition relationship from *Z_C_TRAVEL* to *Z_C_BOOKING*. We also add a new section to the object page by supplementing the UI facet annotation. Listing 5.26 contains the code snippet for the view, highlighting the changes made.

```
[. . .]
define root view entity Z_C_TRAVEL
  provider contract transactional_query
  as projection on Z_I_TRAVEL
{
```

```
  @UI.facet: [ {
    id: 'idIdentification',
    type: #IDENTIFICATION_REFERENCE,
    label: 'Travel',
    position: 10
  },
  {
    id:             'Booking',
    purpose:        #STANDARD,
    type:           #LINEITEM_REFERENCE,
    label:          'Booking',
    position:       15,
    targetElement: '_Booking'
  } ]
[ . . .]
  _Booking : redirected to composition child Z_C_BOOKING
}
```

Listing 5.26: Root consumption view "Z_C_TRAVEL"—adaptation

Finally, we extend the behavior definition *Z_C_TRAVEL* to include the booking node. This makes it available at consumption level. The code snippet for the behavior definition can be found in Listing 5.27; the changes made are again highlighted.

```
projection;
strict;
use draft;

define behavior for Z_C_TRAVEL //alias <alias_name>
{
  use create;
  use update;
  use delete;

  use action Edit;
  use action Activate;
  use action Discard;
  use action Prepare;
  use action Resume;

  use action cancelTravel;
  use function countTravel;
```

```
  use association _Booking {create; with draft;}
}

define behavior for Z_C_BOOKING //alias <alias_name>
{
  use update;
  use delete;

  use association _Travel {with draft;}
}
```

Listing 5.27: Behavior definition "Z_C_TRAVEL"—adaptation

The booking entity is now fully integrated into the consumption view. To finalize the integration so that the bookings are displayed in the service and in the Fiori application, we need to expose the consumption view in the service or include it in the service definition (see Listing 5.28).

```
@EndUserText.label: 'Travel Service Definition'
define service Z_TRAVEL_SD {
  expose Z_C_TRAVEL;
  expose Z_C_BOOKING;
}
```

Listing 5.28: Service definition

From a programming perspective, the linking of the booking entity or booking node with the travel entity is now complete. In the next step, we will test the new development in the preview. To do this, we navigate to our previously created service binding *Z_TRAVEL_SB_V2*, select the entity Z_C_TRAVEL, and click on the PREVIEW... button (see Figure 5.51).

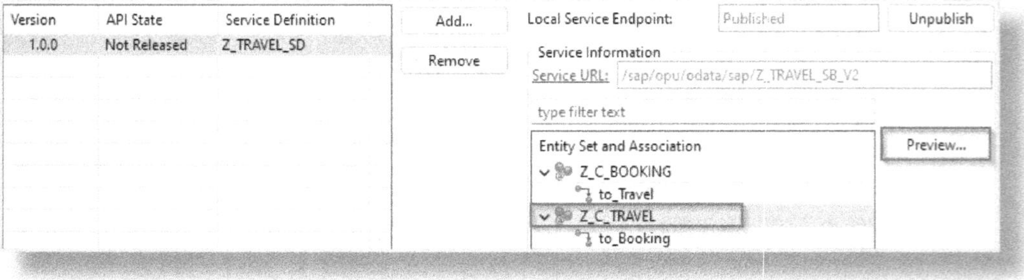

Figure 5.51: Fiori preview

In the Fiori list application, we navigate to the object page of any travel. In our example, we are looking at the travel with TRAVEL ID 7 (see Figure 5.52). You can see that there is now a new table on the travel's object page, which contains all the associated bookings with the unique ID (BOOKING NU...).

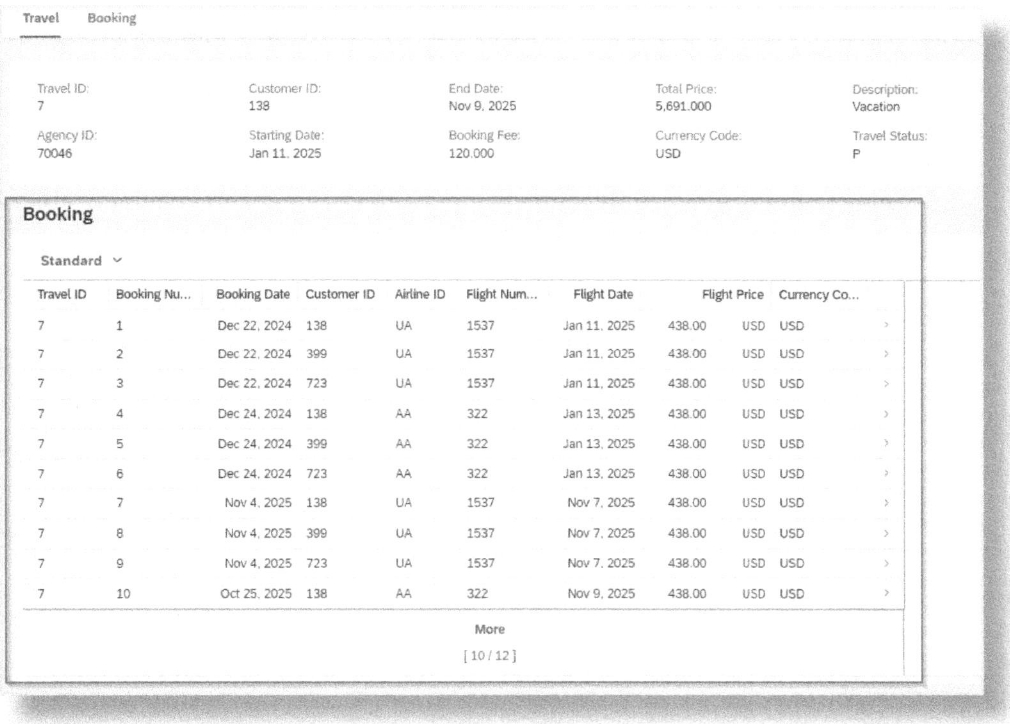

Figure 5.52: Fiori application with booking

In order to create new entries in the booking table, we need to edit an existing travel or create a new one. This also triggers the standard operations for the booking table to appear (see Figure 5.53).

Figure 5.53: Editing an existing travel, including bookings

5.10 Summary

In this chapter, we focused on the advanced functions of RAP. We covered topics such as various numbering methods and the automation of business logic using determinations and validations to ensure data integrity. We explored dynamic feature control, as well as actions and functions for advanced interactions within the RAP model. Particular attention was paid to the unmanaged save method, draft functionality, and implementation of hierarchies, which bring additional flexibility and complexity to RAP applications.

6 Custom entities (unmanaged queries)

In this chapter, we focus on custom entities in the context of RAP—an indispensable tool in an increasingly heterogeneous system landscape. Custom entities serve as wrappers for ABAP code-based implementations and enable data to be obtained from various sources, such as other SAP systems, (OData) web services, and non-SAP applications.

In this chapter, we will go through the steps to implement a custom entity and demonstrate its use in a Fiori Elements application. We will not only cover the technical implementation but also highlight the strategic importance of custom entities in order to effectively integrate and use data from a diverse system environment.

In addition, we will discuss the advantages and disadvantages of custom entities and the specific restrictions that need to be considered when using them. The aim of this chapter is to provide a comprehensive understanding of custom entities and how they can serve as a powerful solution for customized requirements in RAP applications.

6.1 Introduction to custom entities

In the previous evolutionary stage of the SAP Fiori ABAP programming model, we were free to use our own ABAP code in business logic. We were able to redefine the generated *GET_ENTITY* and *GET_ENTITYSET* entity methods to programmatically cover use cases that could not be handled by CDS views and database models. *Custom entities* can be thought of as a simplified form of the previous methodology, where the abstract structure of the entity is essentially defined and then filled with the customer's own business logic using a class implementation.

We saw in the previous chapters that CUD operations in a behavior definition can be mapped in either a managed or unmanaged scenario. In a custom entity, it is always an **unmanaged scenario**, because no reference to a database model can be established here. Furthermore, a second-class implementation is required for read operations.

6.1.1 Use cases

It could be argued that a custom entity is always used when an SQL-based implementation is not sufficient or not possible.

This is because:

- the data sources are not in your own SAP system and are provided by a web service or non-SAP system, for example,
- application-specific performance optimizations have to be implemented,
- you want to use ABAP Managed Database Procedures (AMDP) with your own query parameters, and
- the data has to be enriched or summarized at row level.

6.1.2 Architecture of a custom entity

Let's take a closer look at the architecture of a custom entity, as shown in Figure 6.1.

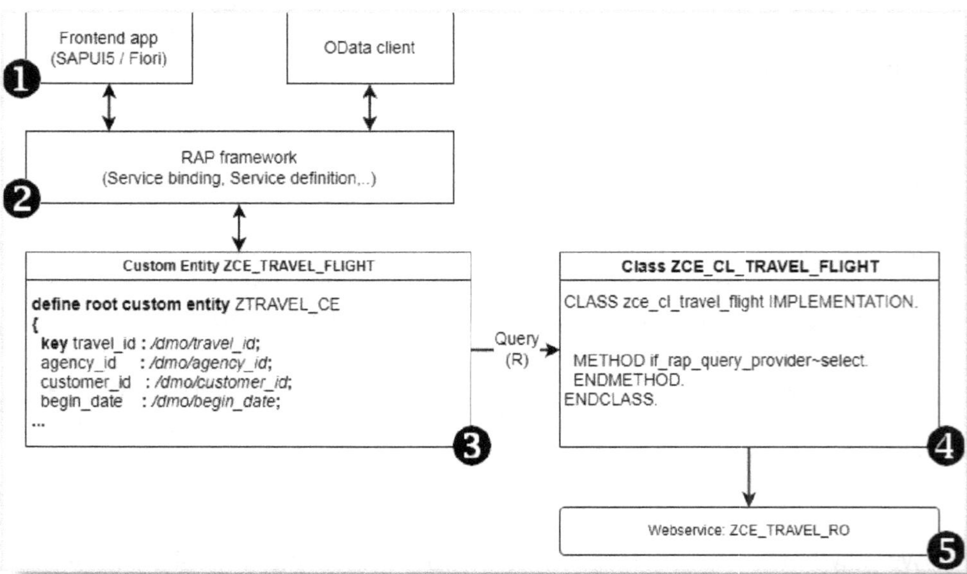

Figure 6.1: Custom entity architecture

As we can see at area ❶, the RAP framework ❷ can be called by various methods. In this example, we have limited ourselves to an OData client and a frontend app.

If the RAP framework ❷ recognizes that a read request has been made to the custom entity ❸, it runs through the corresponding query class. This class ❹ is defined with the code `@ObjectModel.query.implementedBy: 'ABAP:'` in the custom entity. The query class has to implement the interface `IF_RAP_QUERY_PROVIDER`, which contains the `SELECT` method for data selection. We can therefore envisage this query class as a counterpart to the two previous methods `GET_ENTITY` and `GET_ENTITYSET` from the SAP Fiori programming model. In the custom entity implementation class, we simulate reading data from the external system/service `ZCE_TRAVEL_RO` ❺.

6.2 Designing and implementating a custom entity

We now want to consume an existing OData service via an HTTP client and output the data in a Fiori Elements application.

6.2.1 Setting up the service

In our specific example, we will create a separate service binding for the service definitions provided from the ABAP Flight Reference Model. We will then consume this web service in our custom entity and the data will be output in a Fiori application.

To do this, as shown in Figure 6.2 we create a service binding in a new customer-specific package ZCE_TRAVEL. Right-click on the package, select the menu item NEW ❶ and then click on OTHER ABAP REPOSITORY OBJECT ❷.

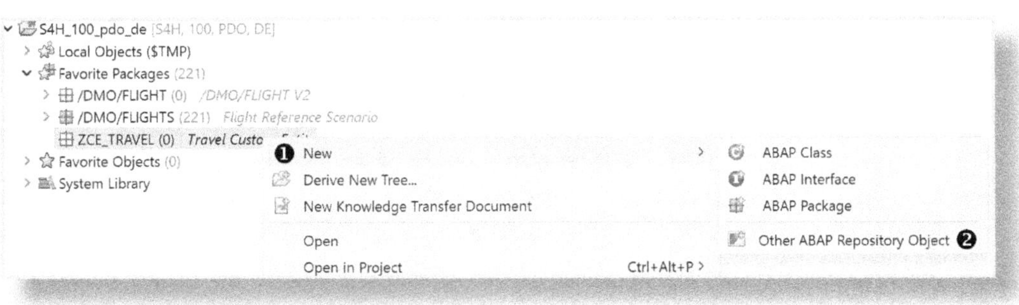

Figure 6.2: ABAP repository object —new creation

We then search for SERVICE BINDING ❶, select it, and click on NEXT ❷ (see Figure 6.3).

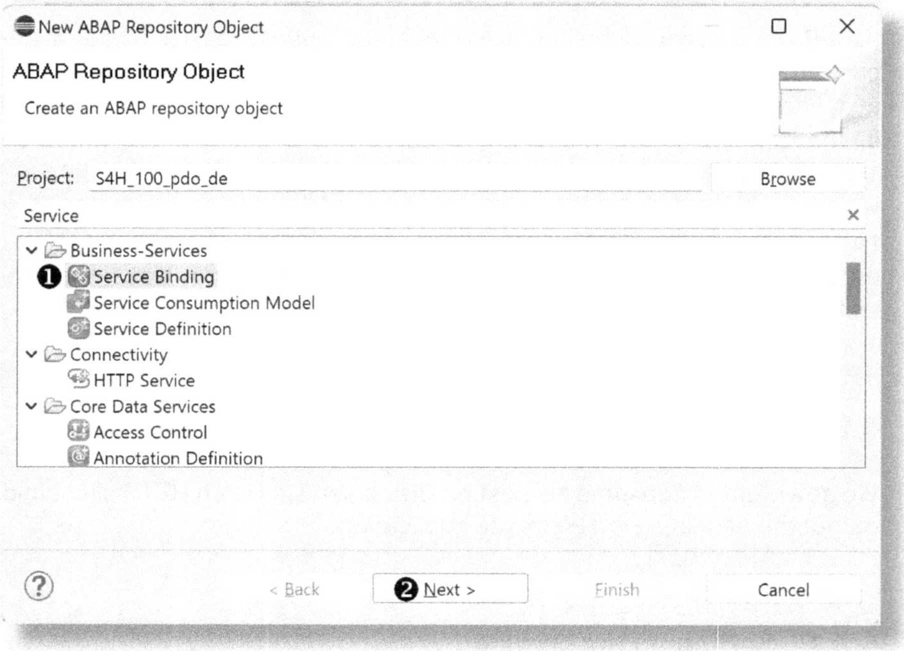

Figure 6.3: Service Binding—New installation

We now fill in the information for the system (see Figure 6.4), with NAME *ZCE_TRAVEL_RO* ❶, and DESCRIPTION *Service Binding Read Only Service* ❷.

Next, select the BINDING TYPE *OData V2 – UI* ❸ and the SERVICE DEFINITION */DMO/FLIGHT_R_V2* ❹. After entering the data, confirm by clicking on NEXT ❺.

! Service definition from package /DMO/FLIGHT(S)_READONLY

Note that the name of the service definition /DMO/FLIGHT_R_V2, from the flight reference model, may have changed in more recent SAP releases. For example, the name in an SAP S/4HANA on-premise 2023 system is /DMO/FLIGHT_R. If an error occurs when creating the service binding, check whether a service definition exists in the /DMO/FLIGHTS_READONLY package. It could also be that the service definition needs to be activated manually.

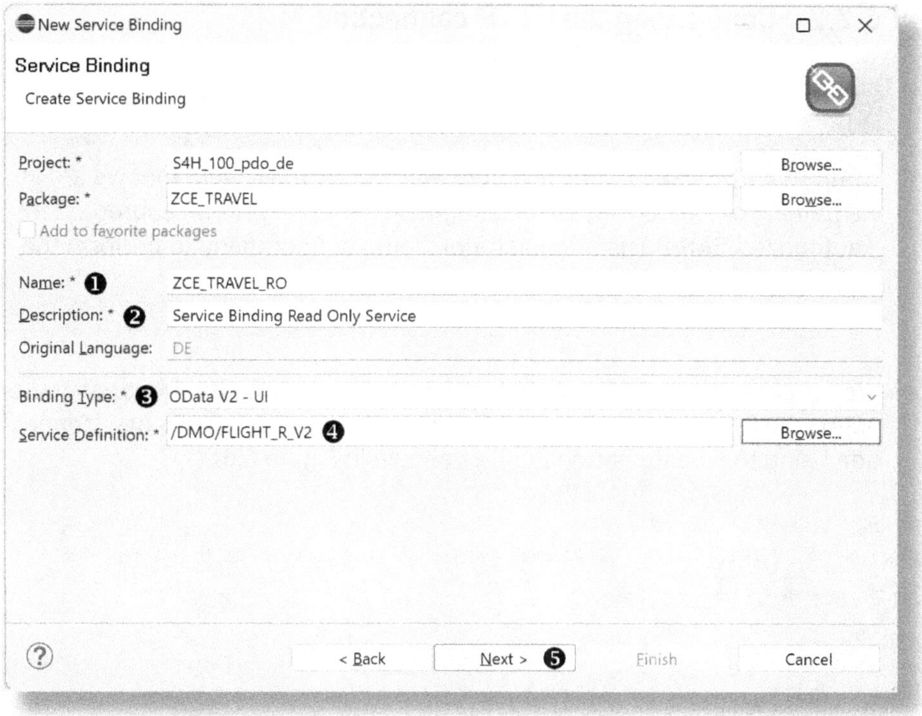

Figure 6.4: Service binding—entering data

As soon as the service binding has been created correctly, a new window opens in Eclipse with the corresponding service binding. We activate it using the button, then publish it using the PUBLISH button ❶, as shown in Figure 6.5.

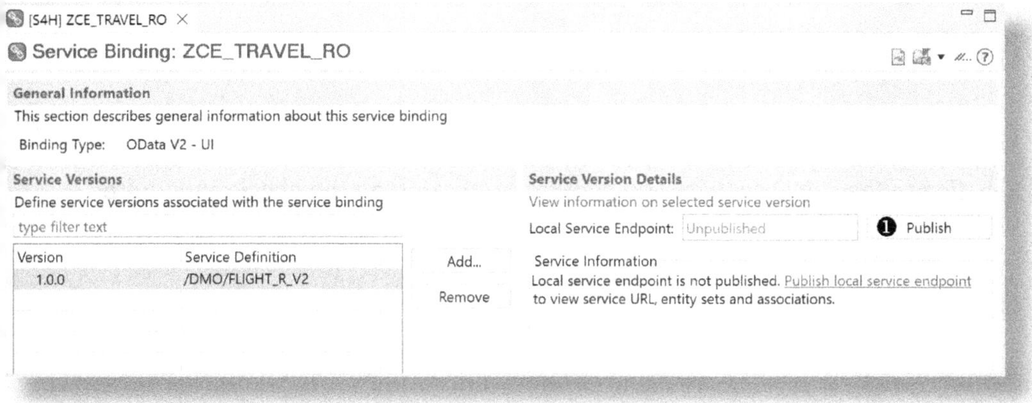

Figure 6.5: Service binding—publication

6.2.2 Configuring the HTTP connection

> **! Creating the HTTP connection**
>
> Before we proceed to the next step, we need to make sure that we are in a training or sandbox system. It might be necessary for an appropriately authorized SAP Basis administrator from your company to perform the configuration shown here.

We now create an HTTP connection for the later call. To do this, open transaction *SM59* (configuration of RFC connections) and create a new connection using the create button (), as shown in Figure 6.6.

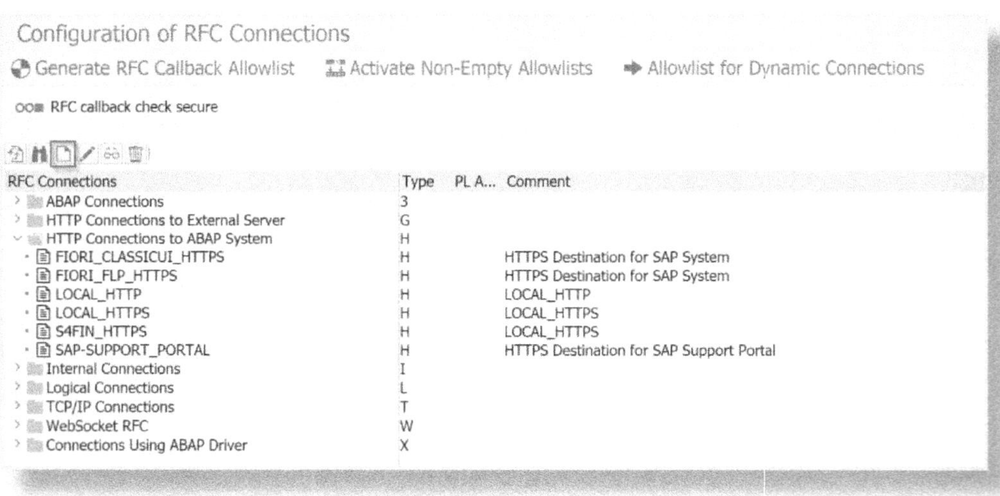

Figure 6.6: Creating a new connection

A dialog then opens, where we define a DESTINATION name for the connection (*ZCE_TRAVEL_LOCAL*), select the CONNECTION TYPE *H HTTP connection to the ABAP system*, and confirm by clicking on the checkmark button (see Figure 6.7).

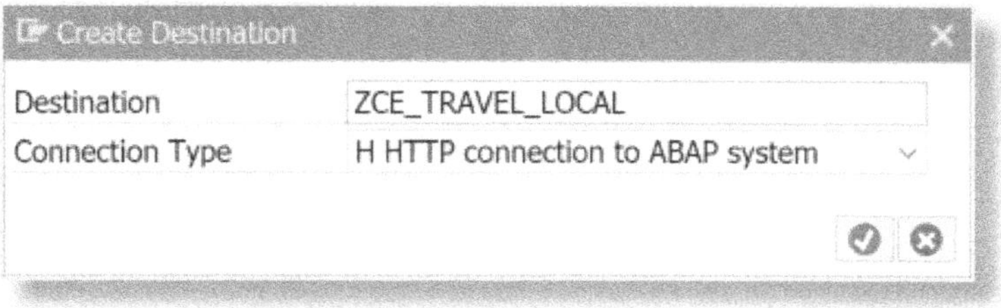

Figure 6.7: Creating a new destination

In the next window (see Figure 6.8), we enter a DESCRIPTION for the destination ➊ and maintain the HOST and PORT ➋ and the PATH PREFIX for our OData service ➌. The new destination points to our sandbox/development system, so we enter our SAP system's data for the host and port.

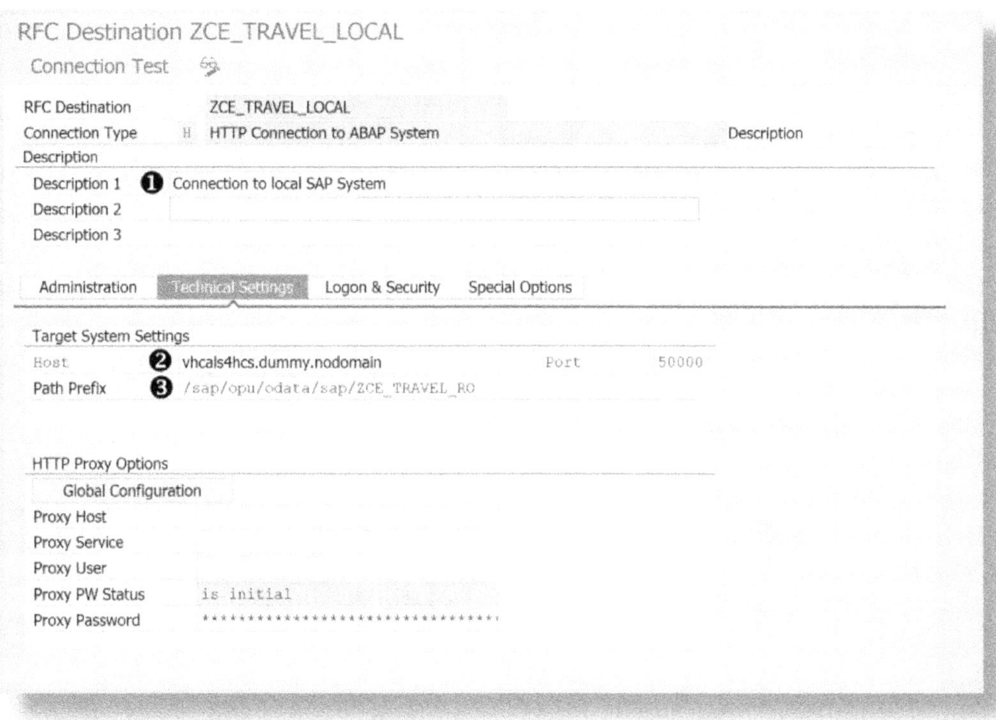

Figure 6.8: Maintaining the destination technical settings

We can then check the connection using the CONNECTION TEST button. If successful, we receive HTTP RESPONSE STATUS *200*, as shown in Figure 6.9.

Figure 6.9: HTTP destination—connection test

We have now created all the prerequisites so that we can use this web service to further develop the custom entity.

6.2.3 Creating the custom entity

Let's move on to create the custom entity. To do this, we need a new data definition in Eclipse (see Figure 6.10).

The procedure is the same as for normal CDS data definition. We search for the type *Data Definition* ❶ in the creation dialog and confirm by clicking on NEXT ❷.

As shown in Figure 6.11, we then enter the NAME *ZCE_TRAVEL_FLIGHT* ❶ and a DESCRIPTION ❷ for displaying the flights from the flight model, and confirm by clicking on NEXT ❸.

Figure 6.10: Select "Data Definition"

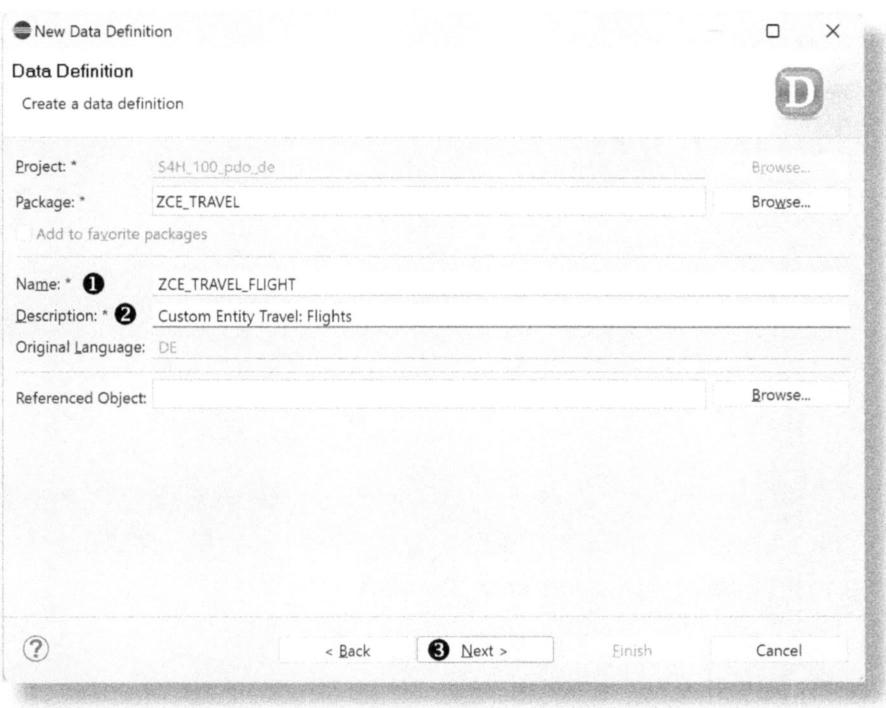

Figure 6.11: Creating a data definition for flight display

! Only use the "Next" button

Only click on the NEXT button for the rest of the wizard, until FINISH is the only option. If you click directly on FINISH in the next transport selection step, an incorrect entity type might be created, and you will have to start again from the beginning.

As soon as a transport has been selected, various CDS template options will be provided (see Figure 6.12). We select the template *Define Custom Entity with Parameters* ❶ and confirm by clicking on FINISH ❷.

Figure 6.12: Selecting custom entity template

In the next step, we define the custom entity fields, including annotations for the subsequent output. The field shown in Listing 6.1 can be found in the Git repository for this book.

```
@EndUserText.label: 'Custom Entity Travel: Flights'
@ObjectModel.query.implementedBy: 'ABAP:ZCE_CL_TRAVEL_
FLIGHT'
@UI: {
  headerInfo: {
    typeName: 'Flight',
    typeNamePlural: 'Flights',
    description: { type: #STANDARD, value: 'ConnectionID' }
//case-sensitive
  }
}
define custom entity ZCE_TRAVEL_FLIGHT
{
      @UI.facet     : [ {
          id        : 'idIdentification',
          type      : #IDENTIFICATION_REFERENCE,
          label     : 'Flight',
          position  : 10
        } ]
      @EndUserText.label: 'Airline'
      @UI           : {
       lineItem     : [{ position: 10 }],
       identification: [{ position: 10 }],
       selectionField: [{ position: 10 }]
      }
  key AirlineID     : /dmo/carrier_id;
      @EndUserText.label: 'Connection Number'
      @UI           : {
       lineItem     : [{ position: 20 }],
       identification: [{ position: 20 }]
      }
  key ConnectionID  : /dmo/connection_id;
      @EndUserText.label: 'Flight Date'
      @UI           : {
       lineItem     : [{ position: 30 }],
       identification: [{ position: 30 }]
      }
  key FlightDate    : /dmo/flight_date;

      @Semantics.amount.currencyCode: 'CurrencyCode'
      @EndUserText.label: 'Price'
```

```
      @UI             : {
       lineItem       : [{ position: 40 }],
       identification: [{ position: 40 }]
      }
      Price           : /dmo/flight_price;

      @Semantics.currencyCode: true
      CurrencyCode    : /dmo/currency_code;

      @EndUserText.label: 'Plane Type'
      @UI             : {
       lineItem       : [{ position: 50 }],
       identification: [{ position: 50 }]
      }
      PlaneType       : /dmo/plane_type_id;

      @EndUserText.label: 'Maximum Seats'
      @UI             : {
       lineItem       : [{ position: 60 }],
       identification: [{ position: 60 }]
      }
      MaximumSeats    : /dmo/plane_seats_max;

      @EndUserText.label: 'Occupied Seats'
      @UI             : {
       lineItem       : [{ position: 70 }],
       identification: [{ position: 70 }]
      }
      OccupiedSeats   : /dmo/plane_seats_occupied;

}
```

Listing 6.1: Custom entity—data definition

☛ Define annotations directly in the custom entity

As you may have noticed in the code snippet above, we have defined the annotations directly in the custom entity. Prior to the S/4HANA on-premise 2023 release, it was not possible to outsource the annotations of a custom entity to a metadata extension. We cannot say with certainty whether this will change in the future.

Once we have defined the properties of the custom entity, we equip it with a query based on ABAP. To do this, we first create a new ABAP class with the interface *IF_RAP_QUERY_PROVIDER*.

As shown in Figure 6.13, we assign the class NAME *ZCE_CL_TRAVEL_FLIGHT* ❶, a DESCRIPTION ❷, and click on the ADD button ❸ to select the interface *IF_RAP_QUERY_PROVIDER* ❹.

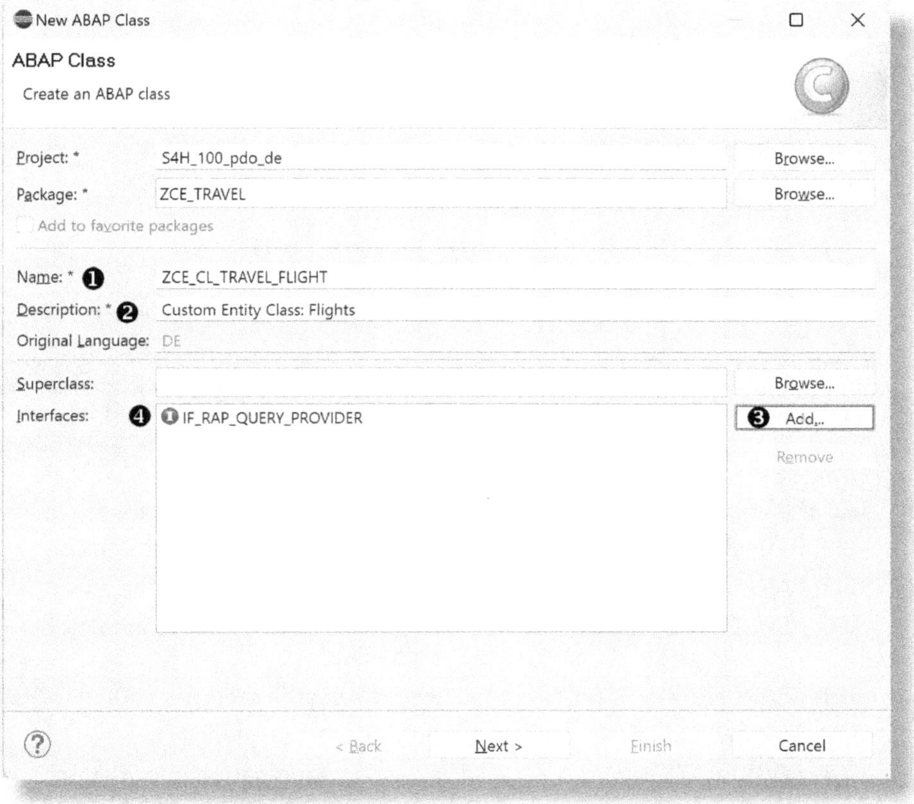

Figure 6.13: Creating a new ABAP class

After creating the class, it is stored in the annotations as a query class for the custom entity.

In the custom entity, a new annotation is inserted above the actual definition ❶ (see Figure 6.14)—this defines the class for read access to the custom entity.

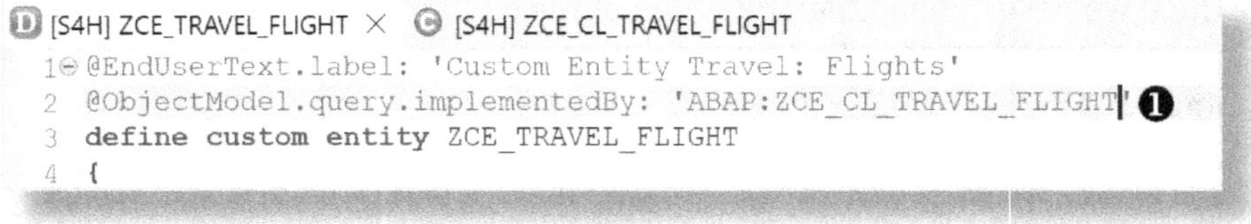

Figure 6.14: Implementing custom entity query

6.2.4 Implementing the custom entity

The IF_RAP_QUERY_PROVIDER interface has the SELECT method, which contains two parameters:

- *IO_REQUEST* for all request data.
- *IO_RESPONSE* for the return of the data.

The IO_REQUEST object instance contains the data listed in Table 6.1.

Method	Function
GET_ENTITY_ID	Provides name of the entity if an implementation is used for different scenarios
GET_FILTER	Provides filter information
GET_PAGING	Provides pagination information
GET_PARAMETERS	Provides parameters for the entity
GET_REQUESTED_ELEMENTS	Returns requested components or entity fields
GET_SEARCH_EXPRESSION	Returns search string
GET_SORT_ELEMENTS	Returns sort sequence
GET_AGGREGATION	Provides aggregation information
IS_DATA_REQUESTED	Indicates whether data should be returned
IS_TOTAL_NUMB_OF_REQUESTED	Indicates whether the number of data records should be returned

Table 6.1: IO_REQUEST object instance—methods

The IO_RESPONSE object instance contains the methods for returning the data from the backend, as listed in Table 6.2.

Method	Function
SET_DATA	Returns the data (paging must be taken into account)
SET_TOTAL_NUMBER_OF_RECORDS	Returns number of lines (paging must be ignored)

Table 6.2: IO_RESPONSE object instance—methods

☛ Return methods

If the IS_DATA_REQUESTED method returns a true Boolean value (TRUE), the SET_DATA method must be called. The same applies to the IS_TOTAL_NUMB_OF_REC_REQUESTED method in conjunction with the SET_TOTAL_NUMBER_OF_RECORDS method.

We will now examine which method calls are used in a standard implementation, and which functions they have. First, we implement a query to determine whether any data has been requested. To do this, the method `is_data_requested` is queried by the object instance `io_request`:

```
DATA(lv_requested) = io_request->is_data_requested()
```

If this returns a true Boolean value (TRUE), the filter conditions are then queried. To do this, the `io_request` object instance accesses the `get_filter` method.

In the subsequent method chaining, we decide whether we want to receive the filters as ranges (`get_as_ranges`), as an SQL string (`get_as_sql_string`) or as a dynamic tree (`get_as_tree`). In our example, we will read the filter values as ranges:

```
DATA(lt_range) = io_request->get_filter()->get_as_ranges()
```

In the next step, we read the required paging. The `get_paging` method is available for this purpose. It offers two further methods in the method chaining: `get_page_size` corresponds to the `$top` parameter in an OData request, and the `get_offset` method corresponds to the `$skip` parameter:

```
DATA(lv_skip) = io_request->get_paging()->get_offset()
DATA(lv_top) = io_request->get_paging()->get_page_size()
```

If sorting is required, the `get_sort_elements` method can be called:

```
DATA(lt_sort_elem) = io_request->get_sort_elements()
```

After we have read the selection and filter conditions from the object instance `io_request` and prepared the data for the return, we send it back to the frontend. To do this, we call the `set_data` method of the `io_response` object. In the last step, we need to set the total number of return rows, without taking pagination into account, using the `get_total_number_of_records` method. This is the only way for the frontend to know whether there are any other entries that can be loaded into the application by pagination:

```
io_response->set_data(it_data = lt_response)
io_response->set_total_number_of_records(lv_lines)
```

Now that we have seen the basic methods required to implement a custom entity, we need to create the `zce_cl_travel_http` class in the *ZCE_TRAVEL* package. This takes care of the query in the previously created HTTP connection *ZCE_TRAVEL_LOCAL*. The program code can be found in Listing 6.2.

```
CLASS zce_cl_travel_http DEFINITION
  PUBLIC
  FINAL
  CREATE PUBLIC.

  PUBLIC SECTION.
    TYPES: tt_ce_flight TYPE STANDARD TABLE OF zce_travel_
flight WITH DEFAULT KEY.

    METHODS: constructor,
      set_filter_options
        IMPORTING
          it_filter TYPE if_rap_query_filter=>tt_name_range_
pairs,
      set_paging
        IMPORTING
          iv_top  TYPE i
          iv_skip TYPE i,
      send
        RETURNING VALUE(rt_data)  TYPE tt_ce_flight.

  PRIVATE SECTION.
```

```
      TYPES:
        BEGIN OF ty_d,
          results TYPE zce_cl_travel_http=>tt_ce_flight,
       END OF ty_d.
      DATA:
        BEGIN OF ms_data_wrapper,
          d type ty_d,
        END OF ms_data_wrapper.

    DATA: mt_filter TYPE if_rap_query_filter=>tt_name_range_
pairs,
          mv_top    TYPE i,
          mv_skip   TYPE i.

    METHODS: build_request_uri
      RETURNING
        VALUE(rv_uri) TYPE string,
      parse_response
        IMPORTING
          iv_response TYPE string
        RETURNING VALUE(rt_data)     TYPE tt_ce_flight.

ENDCLASS.

CLASS ZCE_CL_TRAVEL_HTTP IMPLEMENTATION.


  METHOD constructor.
  ENDMETHOD.


  METHOD set_filter_options.
    mt_filter = it_filter.
  ENDMETHOD.


  METHOD set_paging.
    mv_top = iv_top.
    mv_skip = iv_skip.
  ENDMETHOD.


  METHOD send.

    DATA(lv_uri) = build_request_uri( ).
```

```
    cl_http_client=>create_by_destination(
      EXPORTING
        destination = 'ZCE_TRAVEL_LOCAL'
      IMPORTING
        client      = DATA(lo_http_client)
    ).

    lo_http_client->request->set_header_field(
      name  = 'Accept'
      value = 'application/json'
    ).

    cl_http_utility=>set_request_uri( request = lo_http_
client->request uri = lv_uri ).
    lo_http_client->request->set_method( if_http_
request=>co_request_method_get ).

    lo_http_client->send( ).

    lo_http_client->receive( ).

    lo_http_client->response->get_status(
      IMPORTING
        code   = DATA(lv_status)
        reason = DATA(lv_reason)
    ).

    IF lv_status = 200.
      rt_data = parse_response(
        EXPORTING
          iv_response = lo_http_client->response->get_cdata(
)
      ).
    ENDIF.

    lo_http_client->close( ).

  ENDMETHOD.


  METHOD build_request_uri.
    DATA(lv_uri) = |/Flight?$format=json|.

    if line_exists( mt_filter[ name = 'AIRLINEID' ] ).
```

```
        lv_uri = lv_uri && |&$filter=AirlineID eq '{ mt_
filter[ name = 'AIRLINEID' ]-range[ 1 ]-low }'|.
      endif.
      IF mv_top IS NOT INITIAL.
        lv_uri = lv_uri && |&$top={ condense( CONV string(
mv_top ) ) }|.
      ENDIF.
      IF mv_skip IS NOT INITIAL.
        lv_uri = lv_uri && |&$skip={ condense( CONV string(
mv_skip ) ) }|.
      ENDIF.

      rv_uri = lv_uri.
    ENDMETHOD.


    METHOD parse_response.
        NEW /ui2/cl_json( )->deserialize(
          EXPORTING
            json = iv_response
          CHANGING
            data = me->ms_data_wrapper
        ).

        rt_data = me->ms_data_wrapper-d-results.
    ENDMETHOD.
ENDCLASS.
```

Listing 6.2: Class "zce_cl_travel_http"

After implementing the HTTP query class, we still need to implement the `select` method of the unmanaged query class `zce_cl_travel_flight`, which we looked at in detail earlier. This implementation is shown in Listing 6.3.

```
METHOD if_rap_query_provider~select.

    DATA: lv_orderby_string TYPE string.

    IF io_request->is_data_requested( ).

      DATA(lo_http) = NEW zce_cl_travel_http( ).

      TRY.
```

```
        DATA(lt_filter) = io_request->get_filter( )->get_
as_ranges( ).

      CATCH cx_rap_query_filter_no_range.
        "Fehlermeldung
    ENDTRY.

    IF lt_filter IS NOT INITIAL.
      lo_http->set_filter_options( lt_filter ).
    ENDIF.

    DATA(lo_paging) = io_request->get_paging( ).
    lo_http->set_paging(
      EXPORTING
        iv_top  = lo_paging->get_page_size( )
        iv_skip = lo_paging->get_offset( )
    ).

    DATA(lt_response) = lo_http->send( ).

    DATA(lt_sort_elem) = io_request->get_sort_elements( ).
    IF lt_sort_elem IS NOT INITIAL.
      DATA(lt_sort) = VALUE abap_sortorder_tab(
                        FOR ls_sort_elem IN lt_sort_elem
                        ( name = ls_sort_elem-element_name
                         descending = ls_sort_elem-
descending )
      ).
      SORT lt_response BY (lt_sort).
    ENDIF.

    io_response->set_data( it_data = lt_response ).

    IF io_request->is_total_numb_of_rec_requested( ).
      io_response->set_total_number_of_records( 40 ).
    ENDIF.

  ELSE.
    "Es sollen keine Daten zurückgegeben werden
  ENDIF.

ENDMETHOD.
```

Listing 6.3: Implementing the select method

6.2.5 Creating the service definition

Once the select method has been implemented, we create the corresponding service definition. To do this, search for type *Service Definition* ❶ in the creation dialog box and confirm with NEXT ❷ (see Figure 6.15).

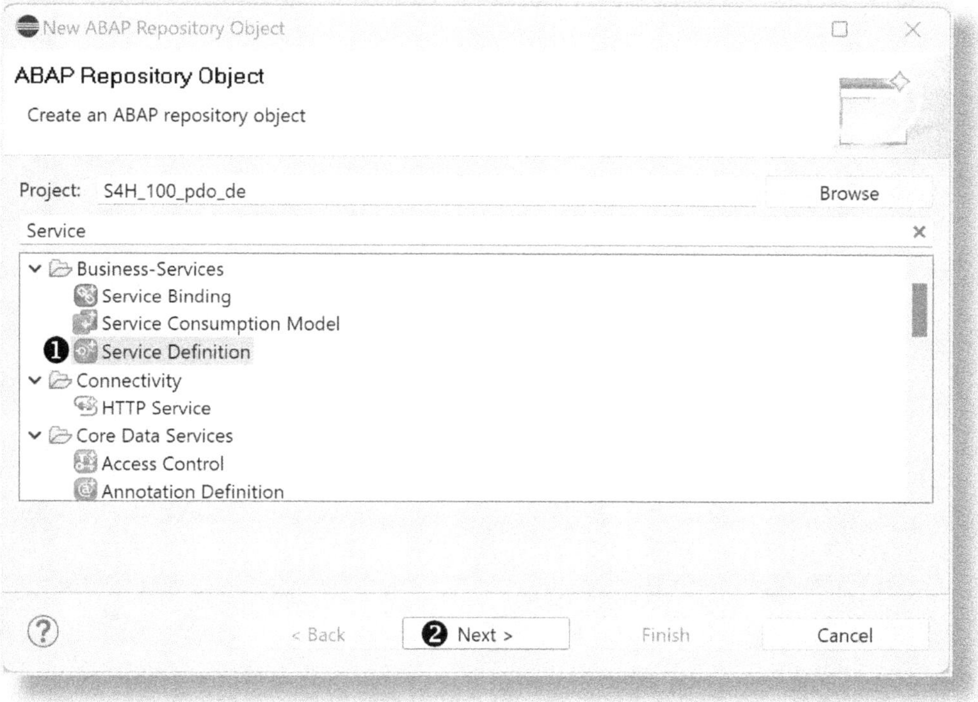

Figure 6.15: "Service Definition" option

In the next dialog box (see Figure 6.16), we assign the NAME *ZCE_TRAVEL_SD* ❶ and a DESCRIPTION ❷ for the service definition, and then confirm by clicking on NEXT ❸.

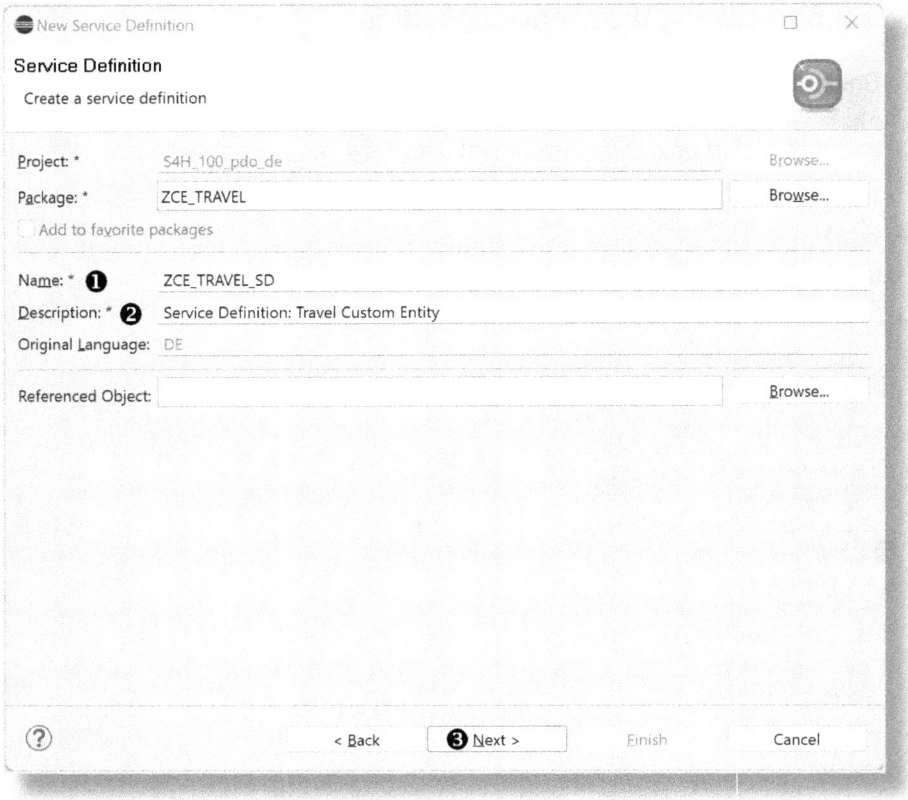

Figure 6.16: Creating a service definition

Once we have selected a transport, the familiar template selection appears (see Figure 6.17). Only the *Define Service* TEMPLATE ❶ is available; click on it and confirm with FINISH ❷.

We then enter the name of the custom entity (`ZCE_TRAVEL_FLIGHT`) after the `expose` command, and activate the service definition via the button (see Figure 6.18).

Figure 6.17: Selecting "Define Service" template

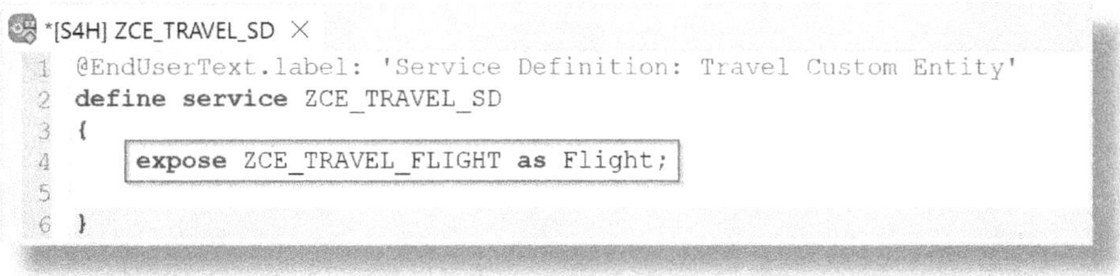

Figure 6.18: Activating the service definition

☛ Alias names can be assigned to entities

A (descriptive) alias name can be assigned for each entity in the service definition.

The name is specified in the following format:
expose <ENTITY> <ALIAS>

6.2.6 Creating the service binding

We now need to create a service binding for our newly created service definition. To do this, search for type *Service Binding* ❶ in the creation dialog box and confirm by clicking on NEXT ❷ (see Figure 6.19).

Figure 6.19: "Service Binding" option

As shown in Figure 6.20, we then assign the NAME *ZCE_TRAVEL_SB_02* ❶ for the service binding, enter a DESCRIPTION ❷, and select BINDING TYPE *OData V2 – UI* ❸. Use the BROWSE button ❹ to search for our previously created SERVICE DEFINITION *ZCE_TRAVEL_SD* and click on NEXT ❺ to confirm.

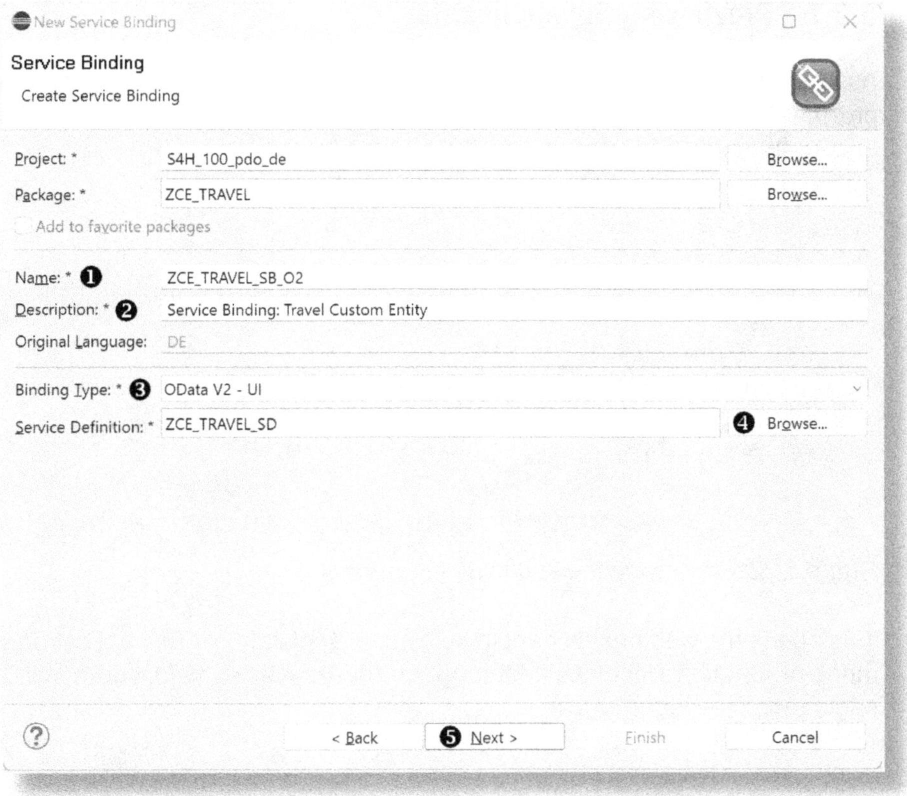

Figure 6.20: Creating a service binding

After selecting the transport request, we close the wizard by clicking on FINISH. The created service binding opens automatically, which only needs to be activated by clicking on the activation icon ( ). If the service binding has been created correctly, we can publish it using the PUBLISH button (see Figure 6.21).

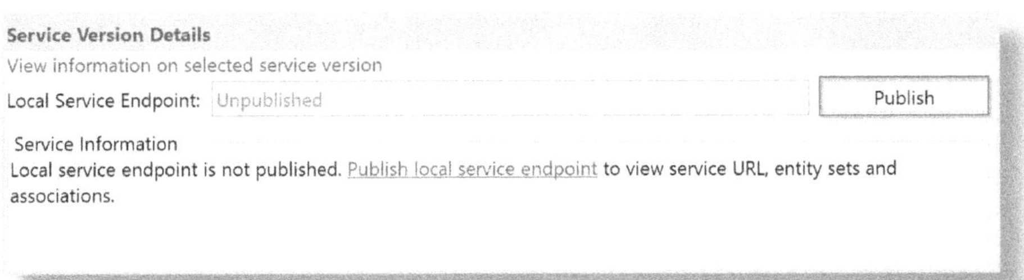

Figure 6.21: Publishing the service binding

6.2.7 Previewing the application

As soon as the service binding has been activated and published, we can preview the application, as shown in Figure 6.22. To do this, select the FLIGHT ❶ entity and click on the PREVIEW ❷ button.

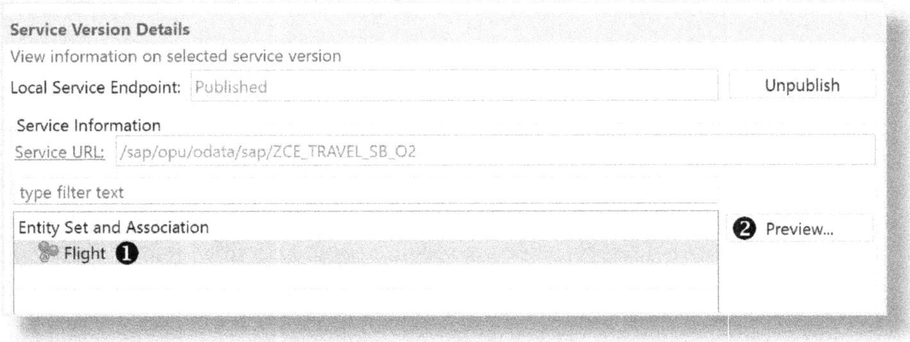

Figure 6.22: Previewing the application

This opens the web browser and displays the application. The application's range of functions includes a filter option for the AIRLINE field, sorting, and pagination (see Figure 6.23).

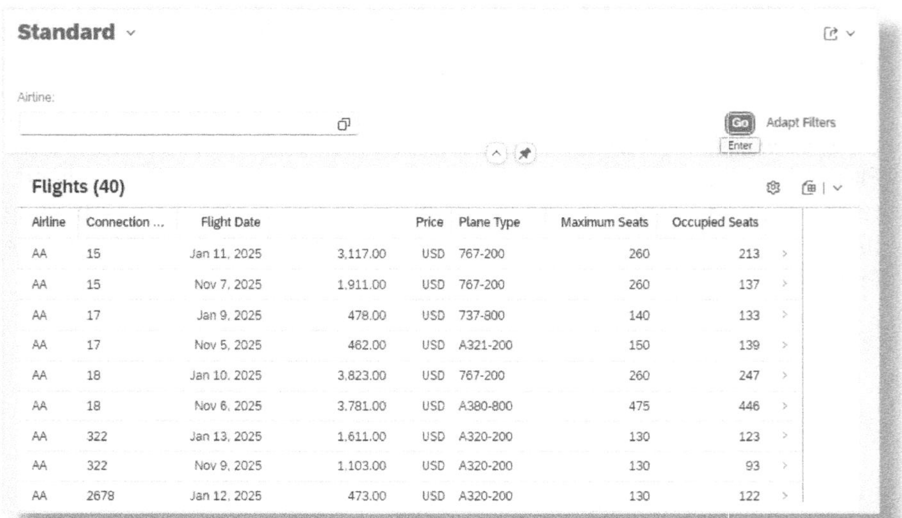

Figure 6.23: Frontend of the preview application

6.3 Advantages and disadvantages of custom entities

Now that we have created a custom entity in a best-case scenario, we would like to discuss the advantages and disadvantages of this concept.

6.3.1 Advantages

The great advantage of the custom entity is the free use of ABAP for the implementation of business logic. This enables complex cases to be mapped, such as the connection of third-party systems. If data in a use case is not usually read from the SAP system, or if it needs to be summarized at line level, then the custom entity is the right choice.

6.3.2 Disadvantages

The custom entity is subject to various restrictions, at least in the S/4HANA on-premise 2023 release, and should always be used as a last resort. It is not possible to use custom entities in a transactional scenario with an OData V4 service binding because draft handling is required there. Currently, OData V2 is the only option supported for CUD operations in combination with custom entities. However, if only an evaluation application is required, OData V4 can also be used in some cases.

If change operations are also being offered, the class implementation of a behavior definition must be implemented in a separate class. This can quickly become confusing for large projects.

7 Conclusion and outlook

Getting started with the ABAP RESTful Application Programming Model (RAP) is a challenge that should not be underestimated. It requires a certain amount of familiarization and a willingness to embrace new concepts and approaches. However, it is important to emphasize that the effort will definitely be worthwhile. RAP offers a modern, efficient and future-oriented programming model for the development of SAP applications that can be seamlessly integrated into SAP S/4HANA architecture.

The aim of this book is to provide a practical and well-founded introduction to RAP. We have looked at the general principles and possibilities for practical application through detailed presentations of the various components and functions of RAP, covering a broad spectrum, from managed and unmanaged scenarios to custom entities.

Thanks to the step-by-step examples in this book, you now have the tools at your disposal to successfully develop complex applications while ensuring the maintainability and expandability of your solutions.

The RAP model is subject to constant change and is continuously being developed by SAP. This dynamic requires an ongoing examination of new functions and improvements. It is therefore crucial for developers to undergo continuous further training to fully exploit the potential of SAP S/4HANA.

Finally, we would like to thank you for joining us on this learning journey. We hope that you have found the contents of this book educational and inspiring and that you are now well equipped to tackle the challenges and opportunities that RAP presents. We are confident that with the knowledge and skills you have acquired, you will develop innovative, future-proof solutions that will add real value to your business and to your customers.

We wish you every success with your future projects and look forward to accompanying you on your digital transformation journey.

A The Authors

Julian Danho is an experienced Senior SAP Consultant and dedicated academic lecturer, and is an expert in SAP ABAP, SAP HANA, RAP and SAPUI5 (Fiori). He is well known for his ability to design and implement customer-oriented solutions.

Julian Danho is also passionate about teaching. As a university lecturer in computer science, he draws on his vast knowledge to provide students with practical insights gained from his extensive experience. This combination of SAP expertise, practical consulting experience, and teaching skills makes him a unique expert in this field.

Phillip Dörrschuck has worked as a consultant and developer on SAP projects for various companies since completing his training as an IT specialist. He is currently working on various S/4HANA transformations, applying his expertise and strategic approaches to achieve optimal results.

With his extensive knowledge of SAP ABAP, SAP HANA, SAPUI5, SAP Fiori and RAP, Phillip develops solutions for customers in a wide range of industries. His talent is evident in the process-oriented development of customized solutions that are precisely tailored to a company's current technical requirements.

B Index

C Disclaimer

This publication contains references to the products of SAP SE.

SAP®, ABAP®, ExpenseIt®, Joule, OpenSAP®, SAP ActiveAttention®, SAP® Adaptive Server® Enterprise, SAP® Advantage Database Server®, SAP® AppGyver®, SAP Ariba®, SAP Business ByDesign®, SAP® Business Explorer®, SAP® Bex, SAP® BusinessObjects, SAP® BusinessObjects Explorer®, SAP® BusinessObjects Web Intelligence®, SAP Business One®, SAP Business Workflow®, SAP BW/4HANA®, SAP Concur®, SAP® Crystal Reports®, SAP EarlyWatch®, SAP® Emarsys®, SAP Fieldglass®, SAP Fiori®, SAP Garden®, SAP® Global Trade Services (SAP® GTS®), SAP HANA®, SAP® Jam, SAP Lumira®, SAP MaxAttention®, SAP® MaxDB®, SAP NetWeaver®, SAP® PartnerEdge®, SAP® Sapphire®, SAP® PowerBuilder®, SAP® PowerDesigner®, SAP® R/3®, SAP® Replication Server®, SAP® Roambi®, SAP S/4HANA®, SAP S/4HANA® Cloud, SAP Signavio®, SAP® SQL Anywhere®, SAP Strategic Enterprise Management® (SAP® SEM®), SAP SuccessFactors®, SAP Vora®, Taulia®, The Best Run SAP®, TripIt®, WalkMe® and other SAP products and services mentioned herein as well as their respective logos are trademarks or registered trademarks of SAP SE in Germany and other countries. All other trademarks are the property of their respective owners.

SAP SE is neither the author nor the publisher of this publication and is not responsible for its content. SAP Group shall not be liable for errors or omissions with respect to the materials. The only warranties for SAP Group products and services are those that are set forth in the express warranty statements accompanying such products and services, if any. Nothing herein should be construed as constituting an additional warranty.

More Espresso Tutorials Books

Prem Manghnani, Seshu Reddy & Sheshank Vyas:

Practical Guide to SAP® OpenUI5

- Fundamental OpenUI5 concepts
- How to define controls for an application
- SAP Fiori applications and design principles
- Real-world examples of how to create applications using

http://5148.espresso-tutorials.com

Robert Burdwell:

First Steps for Building SAP®UI5 Mobile Apps

- Introduction to mobile and SAP UI5 development
- Steps for building mobile apps in Eclipse, SAP Cloud Platform, and Microsoft Visual Studio
- How to deploy apps to multiple devices
- Advantages and disadvantages of using different environments

http://5176.espresso-tutorials.com

Gretchen Horn:

Practical Guide to SAP® Workflow Agent Determination

- Fundamentals of SAP Business Workflow agent types and agent determination
- Example rules defined using responsibilities, ABAP, evaluation paths, organizational data, and BRF+
- Agent administration and reporting
- Deep dive workshops exploring rule definition, modeled deadlines, ad hoc agents, and release procedures

http://5200.espresso-tutorials.com

Marco Verhoef:

A Practical Guide to the SAP® Cloud Connector

- Foundations of SAP Cloud Connector
- Basis activities including installation and configuration
- Developer activities including connection instructions
- Detailed inbound RFC example

http://5509.espresso-tutorials.com

Adam Kiwon:

A Practical Guide to SAP® Cloud Integration

- Understand SAP's Cloud Middleware and the Integration Suite
- Quality aspects for a robust design
- Configure standard integration content
- Reference guide for integration patterns

http://5651.espresso-tutorials.com

Boris Rubarth:

First Steps in SAP ABAP®—2nd edition

- Step-by-Step instructions for beginners
- Comprehensive descriptions and code examples
- A guide to create your first ABAP application
- Tutorials that provide answers to the most commonly asked programming questions

https://es-tu.de/nKfwhx

www.ingramcontent.com/pod-product-compliance
Lightning Source LLC
Chambersburg PA
CBHW071340230926
51846CB00002B/395
9783960124917